Colliding with

Mercury

A Gender Bending Adventure

David Fischer MD PhD

ISBN: 978-1-946600-10-3

DEDICATION

For Mercury,
fellow drag performers
and the staff of the Capitol Garage.

You have all these thoughts and insecurities and then you go to the club... You're dancing around other people, but you're also thinking by yourself...
~Yaeji, Inner Dialogue vs Outer Attitude

CHAPTER ONE

On a Thursday night April suggested we go to the Crocker Museum for their 'Glam Party.' It was featuring a Prince tribute band that I'd seen before (and liked the sexy African-American lead vocalist). But, tonight, instead of her, a stubby white guy was singing, so I spent the bulk of their set anywhere but watching.

Then, during a break in the band's performance (while I was indulging my taste buds at the makeshift café), I heard a roar from the crowd and April came running.

"Hey, Dave, you got to come see this show!" she exclaimed.

And there he was – this thin, young, bare-chested, blond, athletic-looking fella, dancing to Madonna's *Vogue* and looking like a cross between Nijinsky, Hermes and Apollo all wrapped into one. His movements were at once powerful and explosive, evincing primal strength and masculinity. His expression serious, he took a workman's approach to dancing – focused and committed. He was simply a man on fire, generating energy all around him.

"Ladies and gentlemen," the announcer cried, "put your hands together for Mercury Rising!"

Wow, I thought, stunned and applauding. That was really interesting.

Then, a drag queen in feathered gown stepped onstage.

"Now, ladies and gentleman, please give a warm welcome for our next drag queen, Sasha Di..."

'Next drag queen'?! I thought. That last guy was a 'drag queen'?!

"Dave, did you not catch that he was wearing a dress?" April asked, incredulous. "What did you think he was dancing in?"

I thought they were open-chested overalls, I responded. Like he was wearing something modern – avant-garde.

1

April stared, then turned her head.

"He was not wearing open-chested overalls," she uttered under her breath. "It was a dress."

Watching this next performer strut up and down the catwalk, it was more the standard fare I was used to in a drag show (which left me completely uninterested, as opposed to this Mercury fella).

At the close of the drag show (performed in the space of the band's intermission), members of the audience were invited to meet the drag queens.

"Why don't we go talk to him?" April suggested...

Waiting in line, we climbed the stairs to the stage where the drag queens were assembled. I only had eyes for Mercury, who was now sporting a red evening dress, high heels and straight brunette bog wig and looked completely different than he had during his dance routine.

"Is this the first time you experienced a drag show?" he asked.

Well, it's the first time I liked one, I responded.

He laughed full of warmth and friendliness. Given how accomplished he was, I expected him to be cold and aloof; but instead he was warm and inviting...

After a group selfie Mercury graciously thanked us for coming, and April and I left the stage. From there, April made a beeline for the information counter and searched for a copy of the evening itinerary.

"I want to read what it says about him," she explained.

Locating an itinerary we flipped through its pages, but found not a word about Mercury.

"He was probably a last minute addition," April reasoned.

Turning to the stage I looked back. But the band was setting up again, and Mercury and the other drag queens were nowhere to be seen...

CHAPTER TWO

Returning to work the following day felt a world away from the awe-inspiring dancing I'd been treated to the night before.

My interest in dance began early in life, not long after my parent's divorced. I was five then, and among the things my mother took up after my father's parting was ballet. In no time at all my mother acquired such a collection of dance books and magazines that they littered the floors of near every room in the house. I spent hours poring through their pages, admiring the depth of feeling conveyed in the danseurs' movements and expressions, and longing to dance like them.

But any ballet aspirations I might have had were put on permanent hold when I was struck by a car and left unable to use my legs as before. Not long after that my grandfather died of cancer, and I set my sights on fighting that disease. Excelling in academics in grade school and then college, I was recruited by a professor to perform research, and determined the molecular structure of a radioactive compound attached to tumor-specific antibodies to treat lymphoma.

Upon graduating college I received a scholarship to study at the Weizmann Institute of Science in Israel and analyzed mutated genes that cause cancer (called oncogenes). Then, while a medical student, I was selected to work at the National Institutes of Health (NIH), where I developed a means to immunize against these oncogenes, inventing the first cancer vaccine of its kind.

It happened that while in Israel I spent my evenings marveling at folk dancers and the dignity they brought to their dancing. Returning to the States, I took up Israeli dancing while attending

3

medical school, and was invited to dance with several dance troupes while working at the NIH.

But, as in my childhood, my dance activities were put on near permanent hold when I was visited by injury again. This time, though, I couldn't just ignore the injury, because there was so much pain involved. Doctors ordered every manner of test and medication, but none did any good. Finally, I was told I could expect chronic pain for life and would have to just get used to it. But as a last resort I turned to alternative healing modalities and chanced upon an energy medicine technique called bioenergy that got me well. Inspired, I trained in this technique and it became my life's calling. Indeed, I decided after I finished a doctorate in cancer vaccines, I would go back to medicine and help those most in need.

In the meantime, one thing that bioenergy taught me was the more I challenged myself, the stronger I became. As such, it wasn't long before I was dancing again. That's how I met April.

"I eyed you from across the dance floor," she recalled.

She was doing a scholarship herself, working at the Smithsonian Museum. We dated, but our careers were taking us in different directions: April to Art School in Delaware, and me back to medical school in Texas. So, we parted friends.

Thirteen years later, though (after a particularly heartbreaking relationship with a woman named Timina), I looked for April, and found she was back in DC working at the Smithsonian, and followed her there. We married not long after.

That was ten years ago. Now, after a stint in the Northern Plains serving native peoples with the Indian Health Service (IHS), I was back home in California, caring for the homeless and advancing integrative approaches for the treatment of pain. April was doing art – though most of her delicate porcelain figures now hung from our precious canine daughter's kennel, as our dog (Sweetness) awaited surgery for her leg.

Such was the state of our lives that night we met Mercury, who I'd no expectation of ever seeing again.

But April had other ideas.

"I searched for venues in town where Mercury is performing," she said with her usual flare for fun and resourcefulness. "He does something called 'Dinner and a Drag Show' at the Capitol Garage. Why don't we go?…"

CHAPTER THREE

The Capitol Garage was a downtown diner. April and I had visited it once before and liked the relaxed atmosphere, vegan pastries and karaoke. So, that Saturday found us happily back there, awaiting the promise of seeing Mercury again.

We weren't disappointed...

"Hello, hello, hello," Mercury called out, strutting across the stage in a low-cut skirt and eight-inch heels. "Welcome one, welcome all. My name is Mercury Rising and I'll be your hostess with the mostest for Dinner and a Drag Show. The show where you all enjoy dinner, and us drag queens act a hot boo-boo fool for your viewing pleasure. Who's ready to have a good time tonight?"

The crowd cheered and hooted.

"Ladies and gentlemen, how many of you have been to the drag show before?" Mercury inquired. "Make some noise."

About half the crowd applauded.

"Okay, like I say before the start of every show, you all need Jesus," he concluded in an exasperated tone to the sounds of laughter in the background. "So pray with me!" he resumed, joyously raising his hands. "In the name of Whitney, Britney, Beyoncé and Mariah, can I get a GAY-men [pronounced like 'A-men']?"

'GAY-men!' roared the happy crowd.

"Yes, God," he responded. "Now, for how many of you is this your first time at the drag show?"

April and I and about a dozen others raised their hands.

"Well, strap in and brace yourselves, because it's going to be a wild ride," he proclaimed. "We're all men in wigs, so get ready for a hot mess."

April and I smiled to each other, pleasantly taken aback.

"Before we continue," Mercury announced, "there are some rules at a drag show, so listen up. And for those of you who've been here before, sing along, because we know you know the lyrics. Rule number one – Tipping is what?!"

'Mandatory!' came the response from all four corners of the restaurant.

"Yes, 'mandatory'," Mercury repeated. "That means tip these men." He flashed a bare breast. "It takes a lot of money to look this cheap. Reward them with a dollar, a five or a ten, and they'll do some nasty shit for you right in front of your face, and take that money. Or wave a twenty dollar bill in front of their face, and they'll come up to you, and they'll rub up on you, and they'll say, 'Meet me out back for a quickie.' And if you're like, 'Ew! No! Get away!', then just toss a crumpled up fifty and say, 'Go fetch', and the bitch will go right after it. I promise you, you'll never see her again."

"Rule number two," he continued. "The use of flash photography is what!?"

'Compulsory!' the crowd responded.

"That's right," he affirmed. "'Compulsory.' We did not shave against the grain, we did not applied wall spackle and war paint to our faces so you can just look at us. We want you to take pictures, videos, boomerangs. We just ask that you please use that flash because drag queens have what?"

'Five-o'clock shadow!'

"Yes, five-o'clock shadows," he repeated with sardonic grin. "So that flash does exactly what the champagne does – It makes my chin look dainty, my skin, soft and smooth. Yes, those flashes do the same thing to us as those drinks do. They take away the five-o'clock shadows and prominent Adam's apples, so that by the end of the night, I look just like a woman."

"The last and most important rule," he asserted. "This is a drag show, so I need you guys to make all the noise in the world, okay? We're here to have a good time in this safe space we've created. So I need you to be loud and proud, and cheer and let everybody know you're here and we're queer!"

The crowd broke into thunderous applause.

"DJ, are we ready?!" he queried. "Hit it!"

The music started and Mercury launched into his first number. In the limited space he danced in the aisles and between tables, and just the agility of the fella was amazing to behold. His use of body as a vehicle of expression was simply unmatched. I loved watching him move. Even the simplest of movements (like a turn to finish the number) was so in sync with the music as to be perfectly timed and executed.

He was simply my ideal in a male danseur. Everything I wanted to be. Simply the ultimate! The male danseurs I grew up admiring – Baryshnikov, Nureyev, Panov – each brought something unique, riveting and exciting to their dancing. But none had Mercury's fusion of the strength of man coupled with the suppleness and life-giving energy of a woman.

"He has both," April agreed. "My initial feeling about him was that he is male, and sees himself as male, but he enjoys taking on female mannerisms and characteristics. I truly think he is – as Native Americans say – 'two-spirited'."

"Thank you, ladies and gentlemen," Mercury called out through the applause, exhibiting not the slightest hint of being out of breath. "Did you all enjoy that first number?... Yes, God. Are you all ready for another drag queen? Then, ladies and gentlemen, coming up next to the stage is…"

I was expecting the other drag queens to strut around like at the museum and every other place else I'd been. But these danced with a flare that nearly equaled Mercury's.

"Mercury is still the best," April asserted. "He can just do so much more with his body."

Nodding, I was cognizant of something else, as well: I had seen many of the drag queens walk into the diner before the show; then, they looked like men in make-up, toting their costumes in suitcases behind them. Watching them now, though, it seemed like performing as women breathed life into their bodies; they appeared bigger than they did as men – as though embracing feminine energy made them fuller and more alive…

After the ensemble of drag queens had each performed their first number, Mercury interrupted the show to inquire who in the crowd wanted 'free stuff'?

"Let's hear it if you'd like some free shit!" he called out.

Shouts filled the diner.

"Okay, okay," he responded. "How many of you like free alcohol? Everyone wants a free drink, right?"

The medical literature having recently proclaimed that alcohol had no redeeming health benefits, I seemed the only one in the diner who wasn't interested.

Meanwhile, for those who did lift a hand, Mercury selected several to go onstage.

"Let's hear it for our volun-queers, ladies and gentlemen!" he declared. "Now, we're going to play a game we called 'Lip Sync for your Drink.' All kinds of things happen at a drag show – Lashes fall out, hair gets all messy, testicles pop out to the left."

The crowd roared with laughter.

"So, while we were getting lefty in check," he continued, now turning to the 'contestants', "we're going to have you entertain the crowd for a little bit, Okurr?"

Then, after some brief introductions, those onstage applied wigs and danced to Beyoncé's *Single Ladies,* smiling and laughing and having a good time (which I'd cheated myself out of!)…

"And remember," Mercury declared, smiling broadly at the show's end. "Until next week – Eat, drink and be gay!"

And with that, he pulled the wig from his head, proudly revealing a scalp of thinning hair and premature, male-pattern baldness.

"Do you like him more with his wig on?" April asked.

It didn't matter, I responded, as with or without the wig, he still had that infectious smile that radiated joy to all four corners of the restaurant. Indeed, it was a relief that he was less than perfect (and willing to proudly displayed it!), as it felt like it gave permission for my imperfections.

As at the museum those interested in getting a photo with the drag queens were invited onstage.

"Don't forget, folks," Mercury called out. "If you didn't take a selfie, it didn't happen."

As Mercury greeted each and every person with warmth and affection, I looked on with admiration.

"Dave, is there something about you that I don't know?" April asked.

"Just appreciating this guy," I responded. "He really has 'the love'."

She eyed me, doubtful…

Making our way to the exit, a large fella intercepted us.

"Hey, we're doing karaoke next," he said. "You wanna sing something?"

Sure, I responded.

Singing Taylor Dayne's remake of *Can't Get Enough of Your Love,* the crowd congregated around the stage and danced, and I imagined I was experiencing the same exhilaration that Mercury did?

"He says he does it for the attention," April asserted. "I watched a video of people asking him how he became Mercury Rising? He said he was at a gay bar, and there was a drinking game, and he got dared into putting on a wig and sparkly female clothes, and he got a lot of attention, and he just loved the attention, and he said, 'Wow, I think I'm going to do this again.'"

She laughed.

"And that's sort of how he turned to drag," she concluded. "Because he loves the attention…"

Making his way to the door Mercury was passing in our direction. Wearing street clothes and donning a brown, weathered Ushanka-style winter cap, his face was still in make-up, with little flowers painted on his cheeks against a white foundation. He appeared smaller than he had in costume, and though this was no doubt in part because of the present lack of heels (He wore grease-stained sneakers now), I had the feeling there were other reasons, too. Indeed, surveying his oversized jacket that hung off his shoulders and loose fitting jeans, the words 'High School' popped into my head, and I wondered if his school experience was anything like mine? (Moved to a new neighborhood and got bullied by a larger boy who'd grab me by the neck and squeeze.)

April stopped him and said we'd seen him at the museum and were excited to find him here.

"Drag is my favorite thing to do," he responded.

Yes, that was obvious, I said.

Smiling, I recalled something a friend told me – That while I was working on my first book, he said my energies were at their peak, and even though we were separated by near 3000 miles (he at his home in DC, and me living in a rented shack in Malibu), he could still feel that through the phone line, and I thought I'd seen the same in Mercury when he performed.

But sharing that with Mercury, his expression changed, so to portray a certain distance, and I wondered that I'd said too much or treated him too familiar? Whether praise was hard for him to hear, or if he didn't believe me?…

CHAPTER FOUR

A week later April and I were back at the Capitol Garage again. This time, though, when Mercury asked for volunteers for the lip-sync competition, I raised a hand. We'd been sitting in the back, and he'd already selected a number of diners from tables in the front. But seeing my hand still up, he enthusiastically waved me onstage to join the others.

"Okay," he said, cozying up to me with a hand around my shoulder. "What's your name, where you from, and how are you feelin' right now?"

My name is Dave, I'm from L.A., and standing next to you, I feel great.

Indeed, I was experiencing none of my usual stage fright – as though being in his proximity had a calming effect on me.

"Well, you say you feel great standing next to me," he quipped, appealing to the crowd. "Do you think you're going to get lucky, sir, just waving $50 bills around? Because for twenty, I'd meet you out back in the parking lot."

The crowd howled.

Well, I'd settle for a kiss, I responded.

"Ohhhh!" he intoned with what might not have been feigned startlement. "Ladies and gentlemen, let's hear it for contestant number five!"

He opened a pink, fur-lined chest full of mangled wigs.

"Take your weapon of destruction," he said. "They're all awful."

A black wig covering my gray head, the music started, and I did all the things I loved him doing (albeit, badly): Sashaying up and down the aisles; throwing the doors open wide and dancing outside; falling to the ground, then launching into a spat of breakdancing (the latter of which I learned from my childhood friend, Ben, who'd worked as a professional dancer during my college years).

When Mercury called a merciful end to my high jinks, I was out of breath (which surprised me because I thought I was in better shape).

In the 'voting' that followed (which amounted to who got the loudest cheers from the audience), I was selected one of the three contestants to move on to the final round.

"I hope you win," said one of the departing contestants.

But all hope for that outcome vanished when Mercury announced that this next round would be decided by a 'Twerk off.'

"Ladies and gentlemen, if you don't know what twerking is," he explained, "it's the art of shaking your derrière up-and-down, back-and-forth, side-to-side, to-and-fro. It's the bane of white women everywhere, and everybody in the world loves to watch it. Am I right, ladies and gentlemen?"

As cheers erupted from the audience, I stood mortified.

That wasn't part of last week's competition! I thought. And if I'd known about it, I would have never volunteered!

"So, without further ado," Mercury continued, "let's make some noise for our contestants, as they shake that ass for some liquor!"

Naturally, I didn't stand a chance – The crowd ultimately anointing as its champion a young guy who twerked from a handstand.

Concluding the event Mercury announced a 'three song' intermission. Leaving the stage a young woman at the bar pulled me aside.

"You're amazing," she said.

Mercury, too, caught up with me.

"Thanks for playing along," he said, hugging me.

Thanks for putting up with me, I responded.

Returning to the table, April asked what Mercury and I talked about?

"Just some pleasantries," I replied.

Nodding, she narrowed her gaze, regarding me suspiciously...

CHAPTER FIVE

Intermission ended, but it wasn't long before Mercury was announcing his final number. As the music began, I looked to April, sad, having not had my fill of his electric dancing. Then, as though reading my thoughts, Mercury leapt into a tremendous high kick right next to our table, launching himself some six feet off the ground – his knee-high, black leather boots with eight-inch Stiletto heels way above my head. Then, coming down, he all but vanished into the floor beneath him before miraculously pulling himself straight up again. It was extraordinary – A sight instantly seared into my hippocampus...

Like last week April and I stayed for the karaoke after the show.

"Waiting your turn to sing?" asked an older gentleman sitting across from us. "So is my husband."

He gestured in the direction of the stage; but, looking, I only saw a giddy young man of perhaps twenty conversing with the DJ.

I turned back to the older man (who must have been in his sixties) confused.

He nodded, smugly...

Called to sing, I chose a lively tune, hoping it might inspire Mercury to come out and dance.

I'll stop the world and melt with you,

You've seen the difference and it's getting better all the time...

As though right on cue, Mercury did appear. But dressed in street clothes now (wearing familiar winter cap and jacket), rather than dance, he warmly approached a couple at the bar. I called to him during the instrumental.

"Mercury, we see you there. Can we entice you to dance?"

But he remained facing opposite the stage, and I imagined he hadn't heard me.

Finishing the song, I returned the microphone to the DJ and left the stage. Mercury was still conversing with the couple. Earlier in the day April had learned Mercury was in an accident and had set up a GoFundMe page to finance another car. It struck me I'd contribute by giving him some cash with each week's performance and decided to approach him.

Moving towards him, I'd intended to wait till he finished talking; but he instantly turned, and the couple peeled off, as though to give us space.

"I heard you singing," he said softly.

I shrugged.

Yeah, I suppose so did all the other unfortunate souls in the restaurant, I responded flippantly.

He remained silent, his eyes displaying a softness and vulnerability like something I'd seen before, but couldn't remember?

Breaking the silence I reiterated my comment about wishing he'd have danced.

"I worry that I'll break an ankle if I dance too much at this place," he responded.

Nodding, I recalled the lip-sync competition and how I'd worried about banging my leg into the metal barrier on the cramped, tiny stage; then I flashed to his tremendous high kick and realized that given the explosive force he was capable of, snapping an ankle would be easy.

I gave him a couple twenties, saying I appreciated his artistry. He graciously accepted.

"See you next week," I said, turning.

Rejoining April, I thought that was the last I'd see of him. Not long after, though, Mercury appeared, smiling and carrying a dessert plate with a couple chocolate-covered bonbons to our table.

He hugged April and then me. The muscles of his back were supple and seemed to meld into the contours of my hands as I embraced him...

"I think that's his way of telling you it's OK to approach him," April said...

CHAPTER SIX

During the night I recalled where I'd seen the look in Mercury's eyes before. It was after I broke things off with my college love, Bubbles. We'd had a 'summer fling.' She was perfect for me; but my ambitions for cancer research were all-consuming at the time and with the start of the school year I knew I was going back to my relentless pursuit of them, such that I'd be no good for her.

But I loved her and the separation was tearing me apart. So, during the Christmas break, I visited her at her sister's. There, she was on the bed, solitarily placing photos into an album, looking at me sad and distant. And even as we moved into the living room and sat on the couch watching the movie, *Cat People,* her expression didn't change.

See these tears so blue
An ageless heart that can never mend...

"Why do you think people look at you like that?" April asked. "Is it because they have been badly wounded?"

I couldn't speak for Mercury, but, as for Bubbles, yes. She loved me but...

"She couldn't trust you no more?" April inserted.

Nodding, I thought about my beloved, tall, statuesque, dark-haired, caring friend, and covered my eyes.

"And you think Mercury doesn't trust?" April asked.

Pulling myself upright, I depressed the corners of my mouth and shook my head.

I have no idea what he thinks, I responded. Probably just projecting...

CHAPTER SEVEN

On a stroll along the river, our dog was walking with a more pronounced limp.

"Sweetness is getting as old as we are," April commented.

I voiced concern about the impending surgery and whether the problems with her legs might still continue to worsen, especially given Sweetness's inclination to run and jump and push herself?

"A lot of fifty year olds do the same thing," she said, turning and eying me, smiling.

Touché, I thought, recalling last night's antics.

Then, I remembered Mercury's apprehensions about breaking a leg and shared his comment with April. She nodded.

"I read in one of his blog posts that he broke an ankle," she said. "He wrote, 'I broke my ankle, and I don't know what I'm going to do?'"

Wondering about his life, my thoughts drifted to my boyhood friend, Ben, who went on to be a dancer in Reno. I'd visit him during college and we'd go out with his 'showgirl' coworkers; or else we'd drive to the mountains and scale them without ropes. It was the closest I'd ever been to being wild and free.

Then, Ben got married, left the show and settled into a life as a salesman. He never looked back – but I did: I missed his life as a dancer, with the performing and artistry. Perhaps a relationship with Mercury could bring some of that back and fill the empty space it left behind?

"Do you have a crush?" April asked.

I looked at her, confused.

It isn't anything sexual, I responded. Mercury was a person in possession of extraordinary gifts and abilities, but I wasn't homosexual.

I remembered the first time I was exposed to homosexuality. It was when I was perhaps five years old. I had gone with my mother to the LAX Airport to pick up my grandparents (who'd just flown in from New York). As we made our way from the gate to baggage claim, there were two men in front of us, walking arm-in-arm, shoulder-to-shoulder, kissing and overjoyed to be in each other's company. Having never seen such displays of affection between men before, I turned to my mother. She offered only a stern look. But gazing at these two men again, it seemed to me that where these two people were so happy, there couldn't be anything wrong...

"Mercury is probably wondering about your overtures?" April commented. "What you want from him? And is perhaps concerned?"

"I read something," she continued. "That for drag queens, it's nice about the attention they get performing – That people want to know them. The scary thing is, though, that a lot of times, people would be in love with the performance persona, and not want the whole person..."

CHAPTER EIGHT

"I think your attraction to Mercury Rising is on the same spectrum as your attraction to Ziggy Stardust," April continued. "The amazing artist. The way he moves. Similar costumes. Androgynous look. Male body with that female flamboyance.

"And I deliberately said Ziggy Stardust and not David Bowie, because David Bowie later cut it out of his act... He took away those female components and insisted on being entirely male. Versus Mercury Rising, who's an openly gay guy."

I recalled the first time I saw David Bowie. I was maybe ten years old and watching television when a commercial came on advertising the *Diamond Dogs album* and featuring a woman wearing make-up, pleasantly listening to music over a headset, and looking so like Nikki that it shocked me when she spoke with a deep male voice.

Nikki was the tall and statuesque woman my father left my mother for, and who would become a towering figure in my life – both before and after her suicide.

"Was that the first significant death in your life?" April asked.

There were others, but none has stayed with me as much as hers.

"Do you like the strength of him?" she asked, going back to Mercury.

Yes, I appreciate physically strong women, I responded, returning to the subject of Nikki. She was strong. Bubbles was. April was also relatively tall and broad-shouldered.

"I get that," she said. "I also like androgyny..."

17

CHAPTER NINE

April asked a close gay friend and confidante, Carl, for his advice.

"Obviously you're not a representative of the gay community," she began. "But, like, how would a gay guy approach a crush from a straight guy?"

"I don't know," Carl responded. "It is a specific person, so I have absolutely no idea."

"You know I've had crushes before on actors and singers," April continued. "But the thing about it is, all the ones that I've had crushes on, have been internationally famous, so that I've never been in the same room with them or talked to them. Like I never had a crush on a performer that I could just show up at his place of work several times a week, and directly give him money, and talk with him. So you can have this crush, and also mix it up with it, this sort of interaction."

"I would just play with the energy," Carl responded. "But you have no idea which way it is going to go. No idea. There is no pre-written script here. It just sort of is. So, see what happens."

"It makes me think of Dave's high school friend, Ben," April said. "He became a dancer, and according to Dave, he was just an amazing dancer. And Dave and him had this very strong 'bro' relationship. And then the relationship broke down when Ben met his now wife, and Dave didn't like the wife, and that was kind of hard on Ben, so he cut off his relationship with Dave. So Dave has had these strong intimate relationships that aren't sexual with guys."

These were my friends, I thought. Truth be told, with the new friend I'd made out here, Dino, there was something about him that tickled me. I couldn't be sure why? If it was about his being

18

confident or handsome or athletic or cool? Or whether those qualities triggered feelings about my toxic uncle (who was beloved by me and also the possessor of those qualities), and looking to somehow reconstitute that relationship in a safe and healthy way?

Meanwhile, with Mercury, there is something that I love as a dancer and entertainer. But as a straight guy, I've no interest in intimacy.

"I'd say the definitions are really weird here – and constricting," Carl responded. "So go with where your feelings are – and where his are."

But I had no idea where his feelings were, and didn't know how I would?

"Except that he gave Dave chocolate balls!" April inserted, unable to contain her laughter.

"Oh my God, this is really funny," Carl responded. "I mean, this is really fun. It's very open, and it's very inclusive, and it's very not defined. And I like it on all of those grounds. The definitional stuff really falls away. It's not important. And on some level you're there. And you'll see at what level he's at."

"It's funny because here you have two men," April said, "and Dave's like into a friendship, but it's almost like he's interested in a friendship with a woman. Except, where Mercury is concerned, it's a potential woman-man relationship."

"Yes," Carl said. "There might be miscommunications – and there might not. It may just be at an energetic level, and everything is very flexible, and you will just have to see where things go."

"I think it's a lot of fun," he continued. "It is whatever it is. And that's what's fun about it. It just can go anywhere. A lot of potential. Just as long as there's no threat in it."

'Threat?' I thought, not comprehending.

Then, Carl clarified.

"You don't feel threatened by it, do you, April?" he asked.

"No," April responded.

"OK," he said. "That would be the only caveat I'd say."

April harkened back to the early days of our relationship.

"In the beginning," she said, "when Dave and I first started going out together, I liked the fluidity in our relationship. There was a lot of fluidity in our dynamic. In leadership - In that he would lead, and then I would follow; and then I would lead, and he would follow. And I really liked that. I don't think I had that with any other guy."

"It sounds like between the two of you that works," Carl said. "And you were able to express something through that to each other, which is just great. None of it has to be sexual – or it can. But whichever way it transpires, there are no rules. And that's what's so cool about it..."

CHAPTER TEN

The following Saturday April had to go to the Bay Area to help her sister. Earlier in the week she'd reserved a table near the stage for tonight's 'Dinner and Drag', but I was planning to cancel because I didn't want to go alone.

I called a friend, Dino, and asked if he'd see Mercury with me? He responded that he was busy, but perhaps another time.

"So his act is all about being in drag?" Dino asked. "It's not like he could dress up as regular and do this?"

Perhaps, though I'd never considered the question, as there was nothing about Mercury or his act that I wanted changed. Indeed, considering his gifts as an entertainer, I was reminded of something Frank Sinatra said: *"When I sing, I believe."*

That 'belief' I contended was an ability to reach others in a way that helped them – healed them. Years before I'd experienced something like that during a karaoke event at a nursing home in Tennessee. While a talented young musician was singing, I perceived the opening of my chakras and the realigning of those energy centers. In turn, I deduced that when certain artists perform, they extend a healing frequency to their listeners, and I believed Mercury had that effect on me.

"Is he one of those real flamboyant, all-the-time kind of drag people or whatever?" Dino asked.

No, I said. After his shows Mercury appeared in street clothes and struck me as a genuinely gentle person.

"Then, maybe you could ask him some questions?" Dino responded. "You could say that when you got onstage and danced, that was kind of exciting and interesting to you. For all you know, this guy could tell you, 'Yeah, I go down to the studio on these days, and I do my dance routines', and maybe you could check it out."

"Investigate it?" he concluded. "Tell him, 'I have this interest in dance.' Just don't be afraid..."

CHAPTER ELEVEN

Getting off the phone I decided to go to the drag show. Arriving at the Capitol Garage, I told the host I was alone and asked if he preferred I sit at the bar?

"That's fine," he responded, and sat me at the table April had reserved next to the stage...

"Here by yourself tonight?" the waitress asked, warmly.

Yes, I replied, apologetically.

"Awww," she offered, sympathetically...

Mercury passed my table.

"I always enjoy seeing you," he said. "You're the greatest..."

The show began with Mercury dancing a comedic duet with another drag queen named Apple Adams. The two pretended to be in competition, taking turns pushing at each other. Apple seemed quite a bit stronger (and certainly more muscularly built) than Mercury, so that Mercury was literally being thrown to the side. But Mercury's expression never changed – always smiling and laughing.

Near the end of the number Apple lifted her leg over the banister; but when Mercury did the same, his leg got caught between the slats. In response, Mercury just laughed.

"I forgot I'm not the girl that Apple is!" he exclaimed.

And I laughed. And instead of the pained laughter that usually came from me (so that my chest collapses and it's hard to get out), it was an unrestrained, hearty laughter that took me by surprise.

Why was I usually so incapable of laughter? I wondered. Was it the residual of the childhood trauma involving my uncle striking me in the chest? And something about Mercury relieved the trauma that I held there?

Or did it all derive from something much more basic? Like my difficulty laughing was a manifestation of feeling like I couldn't let my guard down? And that laughing now suggested that – in this space – I could feel safe? Here – with him – I could relax?...

CHAPTER TWELVE

After the drag show the karaoke started. I sang songs I was technically good at, but they seemed to fall flat with the crowd.

Maybe it's because the feeling isn't there? I thought. I had to look deep for a song that inspired me.

My thoughts drifted to a homeless patient who died the other day (Struck by a car). In the years I'd cared for him, we'd labored intensively to get him housed, even so much as offering him the equivalent of 'The Ritz' (i.e., a room in the State Veterans Home in Napa). But each time he refused. There was always a reason he turned down these offers: He didn't want to be far from his hometown; he wanted to live on his own terms; he wanted a life that was free, even if it meant sleeping on the streets.

He did it his way, I concluded.

Then, it struck me that I'd celebrate his life by singing Frank Sinatra's *My Way.*

But I didn't realize how technically difficult the song was (with its lack of instrumental breaks), so by the end my voice was so spent I couldn't get out the last line.

Returning to my chair, I felt defeated. But, to my surprise, a young woman appeared, smiling.

"You don't know what happened at our table," she gushed. "A friend of ours just died, and we been trying to do things to cheer each other up, and get to a better place, and just haven't been able to – We've been grieving so hard.

"And then you get up on stage, and you sing that song, and all of us start nodding our heads, and saying, 'That was Chandler. He always did things his way.' And we started exchanging stories and laughing and joking. And it was like you brought all the good things

25

about him back. Like he was right in the room with us, and we were able to smile about him, and the whole mood of the table changed - like some dark cloud was lifted and taken away. And I just had to know, what made you sing that? What made you choose that song?"

I told her about my patient. When I said he was a homeless veteran, she responded that one of her friends was a veteran. But I hadn't realized he was one of the members of her party, so when a young man approached me a short time later, I thought he wanted to sing karaoke and handed him the sign-up sheet.

"No, sir," he responded in a respectful tone. "I just want to tell you that I really appreciate what you do."

Then, he gave me a hug...

CHAPTER THIRTEEN

As the karaoke continued a young couple took a seat at the bar. The woman was lithe and beautiful; the man thin to the point of emaciated, with body hunched and dark rings around his eyes. He sang Vanilla Ice's *Ice, Ice, Baby*, and I followed with the song that inspired that one – *Under Pressure* by Queen and David Bowie. Afterwards, he tipped his head to me and approached my table. As we conversed, the woman got up and went to the DJ.

"She can sing," he said, nodding enthusiastically.

Standing barefoot (like Bubbles would when we walked hand-in-hand on campus), she sang Madonna's *Material Girl*. Then, the two returned to their seats and consumed mature drinks in liqueur glasses. Looking on at this struggling young man and the mature young woman devoted to him, I pondered the role of young women in the lives of young men like this one as well as the one I had been? Do they mother we young men? Love us and give us confidence? And what happens to those of us who sever that experience?...

CHAPTER FOURTEEN

Still at the Capitol Garage a young fella approached me.

"I like the way you sing," he said.

Smiling, I suggested he sing something and offered him my place in the karaoke line-up. He performed a hip-hop number and I told him I thought it was great.

Leaving the diner not long after, though, I was surprised to hear what sounded like someone calling out to me.

"Hey, what's that about, Dave?! What the heck, Dave?! What's up with that?!"

I would have turned and gone back, but considering what happened to my medical assistant (He'd been recently assaulted not far from this location), I stayed focus on the trek to the car. Really, it wasn't till later that I gave any serious consideration to the thought that those pleas could have been directed towards me?...

"I think you need to wear your wedding ring," April commented. "Because you're not there for any meat market, and he might not have got that you had no interest in someone hitting on you from the get go. I don't even know if you know where your wedding ring is?..."

CHAPTER FIFTEEN

After the next week's show a drag queen named CeCe Williams stayed for karaoke to offer a song for (as Mercury put it) 'her man.' Overweight, I hadn't expected much of her as a performer; but her dancing energized the crowd; and now, when she sang, her voice was full and beautiful, and spoke to a hope and vulnerability that reached me deeply...

"I wish other people could have that kind of sense of appreciation," Carl commented. "Because so often it's about power and about money. And there's cruelty. And I can understand a lot of it is based on this kind of cruelty being visited on them, and the oppressed becoming the oppressors."

"I just want you to be aware of that," he concluded. "So that if ugly things are said to you – and I can guarantee that they will be – please don't be real hurt by it..."

CHAPTER SIXTEEN

Leaving the Capitol Garage after another show, I confided to April that I missed the explosive dancing we'd seen from Mercury that first time at the Crocker Museum.

"Maybe we need to see him on a bigger stage again," she responded. "He does shows at Sidetrax and Badlands. They're during the week, but you have this week off. Why don't we go to these other places?…"

CHAPTER SEVENTEEN

Entering the LGBT lounge, Sidetrax, April and I went to the bar. The bartender had facial hair set against feminine features, so to appear like she was transitioning.

"What can I get for you?" she asked.

When I requested a pina colada, she gave me a doubtful look, then took pains in its preparation (Consulting a recipe book).

"Is it alright?" she inquired.

Yeah, great, I responded, drinking from the glass and smiling. She looked at me, unconvinced...

Seated next to us was a middle-aged blond fellow.

"Can I offer you one of these home-made liquor-lollipops?" he asked. "I purchased thirty of them... It's for tonight's fundraiser for the queens."

He confided that he'd been in the closet for twenty-three years before he finally left his 'nowhere' town that 'didn't like gay people' and came here.

Listening, I recalled a patient I'd cared for in medical school during the height of the AIDS epidemic: The disease, having infected his spinal cord, left him not only paralyzed but unable to control his bowels (which, for a man who worked as an accountant and referred to himself as a 'control freak', was a source of considerable embarrassment). Nevertheless, as he lay utterly debilitated in a stretcher within the emergency room, he was without self-pity.

"For thirty years I lived a closeted life," he told me, "until one day I came out and became a beautiful queen!"

I'd looked on in stunned silence: All this misery – all the internal havoc that the virus had reaped – was likely a direct consequence of that moment. That choice. That decision.

Yet in the throes of all his present suffering, he was without regret for having embraced his sexuality…

"Dave, you have no idea the pressure to conceal your identity," Carl told me later. "I lived my life that way for so many years. Where everybody would be talking in the legal office about what they did over the weekend, when they'd ask me, I would change pronouns and use 'they', and never use a name.

"And sometimes somebody would say, 'Well, did she do this-this-this?', and I didn't correct them. And it was horrible. It's a tense thing. Because you're living in secret – with this tangled web, which you have to remember all the parts.

"To this day, so many people I interact with, they make it clear from the beginning that they are homophobic and wouldn't accept me for my sexuality. So I have to live a double life. They can be totally, totally open, and I can't say anything.

"The worst experience was when I applied for a position with the Human Relations Commission. This was a difficult interview to get; you had to know somebody who knew somebody to get it. And I studied the law, I studied the statutes, I studied the court cases, so that I was so up on human relations law and anti-discrimination stuff it was incredible.

"I had three interviews with them – and I aced the first two. I did really, really, really well.

"The third interview was with the Commissioners of the Human Relations Commission, and again they asked me all sorts of questions, and I knew the law perfectly, and I said what I would do and how I would handle different situations, and I cited statutes and studies and cases. And towards the end of the interview, I was really tired, but I felt like, 'Oh, this is going great.'

"And then, one of the Commissioners – with all the condescension that he could possibly muster – says, 'Mr. Veri, what kind of discrimination did you ever suffer from as a white male?' And I so wanted to tell the truth. And to say, 'Well, number one, I'm gay. And, number two, I'm living with a Muslim. So you tell me if there is discrimination possibly against me, or I can't understand discrimination?'

"But what flashed through my mind was, My parents' best friend got me this interview. And at that time my parents were adamant that I not tell any of their friends or anybody they might know that I was gay - Not at that time.

"So I mumbled some kind of really, really stupid answer. It was stupid, because it wasn't truthful. It was off-the-cuff. And I didn't state my truth.

"And I might not have gotten the job anyway. What finally happened was, I called them up and kept calling, because I wanted the job so badly. And I spoke with the head attorney on the commission, and after the fourth time I called over a three-week period she said, 'Well, I'll be honest with you: You were the best candidate – by far. But we have decided to open up the entire process again for other candidates, because we want to hire a minority person.' And all I could think of was, 'Would I have been considered a minority person if I had told them I was gay?'..."

CHAPTER EIGHTEEN

Back at Sidetrax I leaned in to learn more about the blond fella. But it was so loud in there that I only caught maybe every other word of what he was saying.

I looked about to see if others were having similar difficulties, but saw only a sea of happy men, such that it appeared I was the only one with a problem.

"Dave, look," April said, pointing behind me.

Turning, I saw Mercury. Towering over those around him with his make-up and multi-colored dress, he brought color to the otherwise drab place.

But made up like Amy Winehouse, he looked impenetrable, distant and aloof.

"Sultry," April commented. "Probably what the crowd wants."

I sneered.

Why? I thought. What for?

Just then, a squat, bawdy hostess in drag took to the stage with a mic.

"Okay, quiet down in here," she said. "Settle down. We're about to get the show started."

The music began and one drag queen after another appeared onstage; but compared to the Capitol Garage, I found them wanting, and their 'acts' amounting to walking around collecting bills from the encircling audience.

"I think some people who are performing here haven't attained the skills of a more professional drag queen," April said. "They're at that place of, 'I need to do this. I don't quite know what I'm doing, but I'm going to go out there with in a supportive crowd and express it.'

"I just see them in that awkward stage where they're working on their skills, and they're working on themselves and their vision in a place where people aren't expecting so much of them.

"So I don't feel like they're walking around 'collecting bills.' I really don't think drag queens are there for the money. I don't think you make a lot of money off of drag queen stuff. It probably cost you more for the make-up and the clothes. And you're putting yourself out there in a way that might be a disadvantage to you in the larger community.

"I think they're doing it because they have something to say about gender fluidity, and partly about being seen. I think the dollar bills are about the community telling the performer, 'I see what you're doing. And I support what you're doing. I understand it costs money. Here's my contribution.' That's what a dollar bill means to me. To me it's more that they're being supported by the community for this act that in some ways is kind of brave, and getting support for it."

Just then, the bartender who'd waited on us took the stage and accepted contributions from the crowd.

Yes, I thought to the matter of support for those being brave. No question...

The hostess appeared onstage again and announced a break in the drag performances.

"It's time for the facial hair competition," she said.

A couple beard-clad fellas were 'volunteered' and ushered up onstage. One was a handsome Latin type, the other a plainer looking fellow of Middle Eastern descent.

"Who thinks this guy's gonna go home and suck someone's dick?" the hostess directed at the Middle Eastern fellow.

Then, she stepped to the side of a more handsome Latin fella.

"Now, who thinks this guy's going to go home and someone suck *his* dick?!" she declared.

As the crowd roared its approval, I stood infuriated: The first man no doubt had to contend with issues of being Muslim (To say nothing of being gay!), so to watch him being passed up this way seemed harsh and insensitive, especially where it was coming from a persecuted community!

"I think it's more about being edgy then them attacking anyone for their nationality," April said. "That's just part of drag – because it's honest and raw and controversial. They tone it down at the Capitol Garage, but they can still be a little raw and a bit edgy there, too – It's just cloaked in gowns and glamour."

Indeed, the man in question was an utter good sport; shrugging his shoulders and seemingly perfectly content with his small role in the crowd's merriment and lighthearted fun and frivolities...

The next drag queen went by the stage name Carmen Fuego and portrayed a Latin woman who was at once beautiful and seductive, while at the same time tough and indifferent. Her cold stare coupled with side-to-side jaw movements struck me as a character more harsh than funny.

"You often see things through much darker glasses than I do," April responded. "And I think you are looking for things that not everybody who does drag is actually seeking... You're looking for a dancer. You want dancing. You're very focused on a specific aspect of it – which is the dancing. But I think not everybody in the crowd is focused on dancing specifically. And I think a lot of the performers aren't either."

Releasing a deep breath I had to admit that I admired (indeed, envied) this drag queen's courage and ability to assume the mystique of such a fearless female figure (Something I certainly couldn't do). I wondered about the women in his life and if they'd had a role in influencing the character?

Then, my mind wandered to Bubbles and her sisters and what it must have been to grow up with their strong, domineering Mexican father? The mask of indifference that Bubbles would wear at times to weather her father's gruff remarks, and how out of character that was for as loving a spirit as she was; and perhaps out of character for her father, too – who in spite of his macho exterior, treated me with gentleness and utmost kindness – opening to me his home, looking favorably on my relationship with his daughter, giving generously of his time and filling the role of father I never had.

No later than I had begun to relax than she was inserting a needle through her tongue!

"I think she's doing it on purpose," April commented. "A lot of drag queens are dealing with uncomfortable issues, and they have uncomfortable thoughts, and they're working on them, and one of the ways that they're working on them is through the performances. It's uncomfortable and maybe not socially acceptable, which is the whole reason they're expressing it in this situation."

Turning my head away, I chanced upon seeing Mercury heading towards the stage. Still expressionless, he resembled more a boxer making his way to the ring (or gladiator awaiting mortal combat) than a dancer about to perform.

Mercury took the stage, but his act was more lip sync number than dancing.

"It's appropriate for him as a drag queen to be focused on moving his lips when he's performing," April said. "That's a fair thing for a drag queen to do for his performance. You are bored by it because what you're really seeking is the dancing. But it's not necessarily what the performer's going for or the crowd itself is demanding."

I shook my head.

What a waste of talent, I thought.

"So maybe that's what you're reacting to?... You want to be entertained, and you want to be able to get to watch a beautiful dance, and when somebody isn't doing that, you don't like it. Because you're looking for some stress relief, and some interesting dance routines, and I guess that's more Capitol Garage."

Nodding, I still wanted to be supportive and moved forward holding out a couple bills to Mercury. Then, just as I reached the inner circle around the stage, a big fella with a beard grabbed me around the neck and squeezed the sore muscles there.

"You want to be his daddy, huh?!" he shouted in my ear, grinning.

For a few dollars? Because I appreciate him as an artist? I can't do that without being accused of something sexual?

Returning to April, I told her I wanted to leave. Mercury, meanwhile, had finished his act and was standing near the exit. His back to us, he was holding forth with a collection of young men who appeared hanging on his every word.

"Do you want talk with him?" April asked.

What would I say? – 'I wanted to see you dance on a larger stage where you could exercise your athleticism, but that didn't happen.' Or, 'I think you're a great artist, but you didn't show much of that tonight.' All I seemed good for were expressions of disappointment.

Turning to descend the stairs, I passed behind him without a word...

Exiting Sidetrax April wanted to check out what was happening next door at the gay nightclub, Badlands. Inside, she went straight to the dancefloor and danced what amounted to this booty-heavy, hip-hop. Feeling out of place (Not dressed right for dancing), I stood off to the side. Then, a chic-looking fella with pulled-back urban hairdo approached April and gestured to another fella leaning forward on the railing and eyeing her with intense interest.

Turning I went outside to the tiki bar in the adjoining patio.

April followed a short time later, and we left without another word...

CHAPTER NINETEEN

"Dave, why didn't you follow April out on the dancefloor?" Carl asked. "Why did you have that reaction to April's dancing? Why did it upset you?"

I shook my head: Twenty years before on our first date, it had been quite different. It began with April and I attending a concert featuring David Broza, a prominent Israeli musician and well known peace activist. After, we drove to a night club, and talked about a plethora of things along the way. The last was about my father visiting me in Israel.

"He made a stop-over in Tel Aviv and stayed a few days," I said. "At the time I was heartbroken… I was missing a girl from college, and when I told him, he said, 'Look, when it comes to relationships, you go out with a few girls, here and there, and when you get tired of all that, you marry someone. You just get tired of that kind of thing after a while. You get lonely, so you settle down, and that's what happens.' I remember listening and experiencing this sense of complete and utter disbelief. 'You get 'lonely'?' I thought. 'Are you kidding?' I'd put my faith in things he'd told me. He said I'd be happier when I got into medical school, and I'd find somebody new. 'You'll have to beat them off you with a broom,' he said. So when he told me this about picking someone because you're 'lonely', I felt like someone had just pulled the biggest practical joke on me in the world."

April sank in the car seat.

"Sometimes that's the hand you're dealt," she uttered distantly.

I thought my recounting of these events had ruined the evening.

But arriving at the club, rather than dispirited, April appeared anxious to dance. Following her to the dancefloor, she lost herself in the music, looking in harmony with everything around her.

A round of slow songs followed, and she took my hand and led me to the bar.

"Have you ever had Arak?" she asked. "It's a licorice liqueur made from the anise plant. We used to grow it on the kibbutz. I remember nibbling on it when I was little."

She gazed out.

"I like this place," she said.

I followed her back on the dancefloor. But, not long after, a second round of slow songs followed. She looked at me.

"Well?" she asked.

"Come here," I said.

Pulling her close, contractions darting from her solar plexus, and, holding her, it felt as though her ribs were tightly packed.

She carries a lot of sadness, I thought. Like me.

Then, she laid her head on my shoulder and draped herself around me...

So having not pursued her now onto the dancefloor at Badlands left me to wonder what had become of me? Why she seemed alive – and I was dead?

"Why weren't you dancing with her?" Carl asked. "Why didn't you feel alive?"

There was every number of excuses – Feeling old, April's dancing, the clothes I was wearing, the 'daddy' comment.

"I wish you would have looked that 'daddy' remark in the face," Carl responded, "and said, 'I'm about to disprove that in every way,' and joined April on the dancefloor.

"You just need to wear your jeans," April added, "and a short sleeve shirt and then you would look just right."

But I was frustrated. Just the day before April had taken a photo of me sitting with the cat that showed an expanding bald spot on the back of my head. I'd have been the only guy on the dancefloor with gray hair (I couldn't use hair dyes because they burned my scalp), not to mention a bald spot. I felt like, What was I doing there? I mean, can't I leave these young people alone? Why do they have to be around an old man at this place that they congregate to go dancing? For that matter, why would a young guy like Mercury want to associate with me?

"Dave, you're going to get hurt here," Carl responded. "I'm concerned. I'm concerned about your sensibility here. You're going to get hurt. Mercury is many things to many people. And that's part of being a drag queen. And apparently Mercury does it really well and has these people really enthralled. So please be careful here. You're going to be really hurt if you're seeing this as real."

But the only thing I see as real is this very talented person whose career I'd like to help advance.

And I want him to be happy – I don't want things to be hard for him. So, if I can help, I'd like to. And the reason I don't tell him that directly is because it all seems 'heavy', so I've been keeping it to myself.

April turned to Carl.

"Does he have it bad or what?" she asked, smiling.

"Yes," he responded. "I think you have created a real narrative around this drag queen for whom – from my experience – I can tell you it's a much tougher world than you think."

I flashed to a night at the Capitol Garage that a homeless man entered the diner during one of Mercury's performances; when the man began approaching patrons seated at the different tables, Mercury intercepted him and escorted him out, seemingly without missing a step in his dance number.

So it wasn't like I didn't know Mercury was tough; I just want to do my part to help this person who appears in something of a vulnerable position.

"But you don't know if Mercury's aspirations are to break out of the drag world," Carl said. "You don't know anything about him really."

"We don't even know his name," April added.

I didn't want him to 'break out the drag world.' Really, I wanted him to advance that world – Bring it into 'the new' – by showing guys like me (who'd previously been repulsed by drag shows) what drag could be.

"He is fabulous," April affirmed. "The way he can move his body. I like him."

"But do you know anything about his aspirations in life?" Carl asked. "Because you've just created a huge goal for this person who may not have that goal."

"I think he's quite invested in the life of a drag queen," April responded. "I think he has created his world around being a drag queen, and he wants to be the most successful drag queen, who wins competitions, and gets recognition as a drag queen. I think one of the reasons he is of limited financial means is because that's his focus. That's what he wants. And he is sacrificing financial stability because I think that's a pretty tough road to walk."

"I'm sure it is," Carl agreed. "But who knows what world he wants? There's a lot of supposition in the assumptions you're making, Dave, and it really concerns me. He sounds like a nice guy, but I'm sure he's had to be very, very tough."

"And I don't know," he added. "Is he exploiting you at all? Do you get that feeling?"

Not at all, I responded. The last time I tried to give him a contribution after the show, all he wanted to do was tell me about his wig. I had to all but push it on him.

"I think he pays more attention to me and Dave because Dave gives him the extra money," April said. "So he definitely says hello when we show up. But that's about it. He Approaches lots of different people and flirts with them. Before the show. After the show. During the show. He'll come and give you a moment of his attention while he takes your dollar bill, or whatever. But that's it. I haven't seen him do anything other than that with Dave. It's just a little bit of attention. And the smiles. And flirt on the floor while he's watching her show."

"Well, please don't let him have your dog's room," Carl said. "I'm concerned. I'm concerned that you're going to get hurt here somehow. And I'm not sure how?"

"You really seem emotionally invested," he asserted. "And I think one should never be emotionally invested with a drag queen unless you're another drag queen."

"Yeah, he's very sweet," April said. "But if you read his social media, the comments are a little biting sometimes."

"The comments can be unbelievably biting," Carl added. "Just cutting people down and destroying careers."

I shrugged.

So many doors have been slammed in my face over the past years, I responded, flippantly. One more? – What the hell.

"But you're so emotionally invested in this one," April insisted.

"Yes, this feels emotionally invested," Carl added. "I'm agreeing with April. Be careful. Because your emotions, I would say, there's a 90% chance that you're going to get trampled. Because I agree with April that his really nice persona has to be measured against the very real put downs in the social media. It's a world that has a lot of snapping in it... Snap comments and cutting people down. And if you're aware of that and you're fine with that, OK. But there's an aspect of it that would really turn you off with your idealism."

I am so open to this not working, I responded not unsarcastically. Where I'm a straight man facing concerns from people like my wife about wanting a relationship with a gay man... Well, if it didn't work out, that would be fine.

"As long as you're emotionally OK with it," Carl said. "I'm just thinking when you see other sides of him and you have insults hurled at you that are really hurtful and stinging and biting... Well, the daddy comment is really mild compared to what some people could say."

"The hurt would be being told you're irrelevant," he concluded...

CHAPTER TWENTY

April offered a different take on the 'daddy' comment.

"Maybe they're protecting?" she said. "I think there is that at times when it comes to relationships with an older guy that has money and a younger guy that doesn't. That there's a power-play there, and maybe it's a little bit frowned upon. So that could be part of why there might be this cultural bias against older guys with younger guys."

I flashed to that night at the Capitol Garage with the older fella gesturing to his young husband and feeling ill-at-ease.

"Yeah," April responded. "Young, flaming female guy who is gay, and the husband who is quite a bit older. Yeah, it was so typical – 'Daddy.'"

So I take it that's the perception of what older guys do?... They look for someone for whom they could be daddy?

"Well, you like Mercury's body," she responded. "The bodies of young guys are better than the bodies of older guys. It's just the way it is."

"That's why we should probably stay with the Capitol Garage," she asserted, "where we can watch a cabaret show, and we can give Mercury dollars to support him. There you can do that and be heterosexual.

"Because the moment you step into Sidetrax for a drag show – on a static Sunday night at a gay bar – then you are gay! And if you're doing something like that, you're making a pass.

"They assumed you were gay. They did not assume you were heterosexual. They were going to assume you were a gay guy, and he was turning you on."

And that's what drag is? I asked. Turning someone on?

"Yes, it's sexual. It's like going to a strip club. It's a little like a go-go dancer. It's a sexualized dance for evening entertainment."

But now that I've been introduced to it – and to drag queens – I think there's more to it. For most it seemed an artistic endeavor, for which they put a lot into. There's questioning of gender, and gender roles and identity. So that there's more to it than something like a strip show.

"I've never been to strip club," she responded, "but I've seen the movie *Flashdance* – where the character is a striptease dancer and she put a lot of creativity into her routines at the strip club. So I think it's like that. So you can be a more sultry or a more artistic dancer. And I think Mercury is a really great dancer, and he's kind of fluid, in that he's bucking the system of wearing pads and looking female. He is male.

"He's also very slender, so that he has almost no shoulders. So that his body is androgynous. But at the same time his arm muscles are pretty developed in the way that most people would attribute to males and what male muscles do, even if you're a really strong woman.

"So he's androgynous towards male, and he likes to wear female clothes. Like with his makeup, he's not trying to be a beautiful woman. His makeup is all theatrical.

"What he makes me think about is, when you have gender roles between males and females, women can wear tone down clothes, but they can also wear clothes that are sparkly, and with different designs and some very interesting clothes. Guys not so much – Guys are supposed to wear a more toned down clothes. And to me, what he saying is, 'Well, I want to wear those kinds of clothes. I want to wear something sparkly. I want to wear something colorful. I want to wear something sexy. I want to wear something interesting. I want to be a guy. I am a guy. And I'm OK with being a guy. I'm not trying to be a female. I want to be able to wear these attractive and eye-catching clothing that usually only females are allowed to wear in our society.' That's what I'm getting from him. It's not just a female when he comes on stage, he's also putting on a lot of male mannerisms. So he is gender fluid in his appearance. And, as an artist, he's questioning gender roles - both to himself and to his audience. That's what I'm reading.

"Some of the other drag queens take it further, because they are altering their bodies. Not permanently, not surgically, but with their padding. Kind of transform into female bodies, so that they are putting on the female shape – whereas he is keeping his male shape that he has. And it's almost like he saying, 'I'm a guy. Look at me, I

44

am a guy. I am not changing my body. But I want you to pay attention to me the way you would a female who is putting on these kinds of eye-catching clothes…'"

April commented that Mercury was very popular at Sidetrax.

"He has all kinds of followers in there," she said.

He's a great dancer, I responded. To my mind he was the only dancer there. All the rest were just collecting bills.

"I thought you were kind of jealous," she responded. "That Mercury wasn't flashing you with a smile. If he would've smiled at you and said hello, you would have been over the moon."

It's not about being infatuated, I said. It's about appreciating his talent and wanting to support him.

"That would have given you a chance," she responded. "To talk to him."

Perhaps, but I still feel a certain reticence. Look what happened that first night when I said something to him at the Capitol Garage.

"So you're saying that you're star-struck, rather than love sick?" she inquired. "Because there was this entourage around him, and you usually get to interact with him, and this time he didn't say anything to you."

Truth is, I felt sad for him. It seemed he had to wear this sultry persona that I don't particularly think is him.

"But what if he wants to be sultry? What if that's part of what he wants?"

Sure, if that's what he wants to explore – if that's important to finding himself – then by all means.

Still, when I'm with him, I experience this ease and sweetness.

But in that moment, I realized she was right, and I was pushing my thoughts on him, and didn't want to hold him back…

CHAPTER TWENTY-ONE

Reflecting on the episode days later, I felt even more disappointment: April had been probably drugged that evening, and I'd let my personal hang-ups get in the way of recognizing it.

"That lollipop from the blond guy at the bar," I told her. "It was probably laced with ecstacy. That's probably why you felt compelled to dance that way."

"Did someone give me a lollipop?" she asked.

Her lack of memory of the incident further confirmed my suspicion.

"I remembered that I wanted to dance," she said. "And I was upset that you were not in on the program.

"I was feeling more annoyed at you that you were loving the way that Mercury danced, and then when I try to be suggestive, you were like, 'No.' I wasn't allowed to dance like that. That's how I remember it. But I don't actually remember the lollipop."

"But it could be," she admitted. "I was euphoric, so my memories are distorted."

Then, she smiled impishly.

"I guess I broke the cardinal rule," she said. "Never take candy from a stranger."

We laughed and decided to give Badlands another try.

But this time, getting on the Badlands dancefloor, it felt like being surrounded by a lot of guys performing ritual mating behaviors in territorial rutting displays.

This isn't for me, I determined. I'm about making room for people – bringing people in – Not fighting for a one square foot piece of real estate on the dancefloor!

In other cities I'd enjoyed the gay nightclubs, because I found them more friendly and less testosterone driven than the straight clubs. But here it felt like we were being 'butted' out of the way with exhibitions of twerking, which for me amounted to performing a sex act on a crowded dancefloor.

"These are places where people can be very open about being in a gay relationship," April insisted. "So it's like a safe place where the community expresses itself."

Just then, a mixed gay couple began dancing next to us, and when the African American partner experienced the same 'butting' I had, he just smiled and gently and good-naturedly swatted at the offender's tush a couple times and it was over.

But despite his mature example, I still felt too inhibited than to do the same.

"I guess the urban club scene just isn't for me," I told April. "And I've become too old or old-fashioned or family-oriented or something."

But April thought I was being judgmental.

"They're registering you as competition," she asserted. "As a male. 'Are you going to play?'…"

CHAPTER TWENTY-TWO

A straight person entering the drag world was trying to gain acceptance.

"Go with the flow," she was told.

But having gotten involved with an older drag show attendee, it turned out he was extraordinarily well-endowed, and in the intimate act that followed, she appeared less than comfortable...

Awakening from the dream, I told April.

"Was he intentionally making her uncomfortable?" she asked.

Let's say it looked like she was having a difficult time 'receiving' him.

More to the point, I thought the night's experiences had triggered me.

"What do you mean?" she asked.

Sex with men, I responded, matter-of-factly.

"Oh, about who would be going in?" she responded, laughing. "Who would be the pitcher, and who would be the catcher?... You would want to be the pitcher, right?"

Neither, I said. Mercury may be my alter ego in dance, but it doesn't mean I wanted to have sex with him.

"What do you mean by 'alter ego'?" she asked.

To dance uninhibited as he does. To own the stage. To be the source of so much joy and fun.

"So you want to have a stage presence like that?" she asked. "Then, how come when you sing, you're not engaging the crowd."

How would I do that?

"Look at them. Pay attention to them the way that entertainers do – who react to the crowd as they're singing and dancing. That's what Mercury does."

I shook my head.

I don't think I'm good enough, I responded.

"So you're hiding?" she asked.

I'd prefer to say being modest.

"But don't you know people enjoy the energy of having other people interact with them?" she asked. "And they will actually forgive you if you're not perfect.

"I think you're singing is definitely good enough to be proud of, and interact with the crowd. And the crowd would enjoy you more, and give you more energy if you were engaged with them.

"I don't think you have to hide. You have nothing to hide. You sing in tune. You know the words. You do it in the style of the artist."

"The people who go up and everybody cringes are the people who sing off key," she continued. "You never sing off key. So maybe you don't hit the high notes sometimes – because your voice isn't trained - but I'm sure you would if your voice was trained.

"So you have nothing to be embarrassed about. You should own the stage, like when you do your bioenergy and book talks.

"Do your movements. Bring them Mercury. Be a showman. Where people want to be entertained, I think you could go in with attitude."

She hesitated.

"When you go up on the stage," she resumed, "for some reason, you sing for yourself. You become rather closed and very focused on the singing. I always thought that was because you were focused on the singing, and didn't know it was because you were hiding.

"It's funny that you go out there to be in front of everybody, and then you hide."

"Don't go up there to hide," she concluded, spiritedly. "Just be yourself. Bring all you have to being up there and show it…"

CHAPTER TWENTY-THREE

The next Saturday at the Capitol Garage brought a ruckus crowd. Midway through the show (when Mercury asked for takers in the Lip Sync for your Drink competition), the source of all this 'merriment' (i.e., mayhem) availed itself in the form of a woman celebrating her birthday.

"Fuck yeah," was her response to the question of whether she was going to win the competition, to which the whole of the back of the diner responded with unrestrained, boisterous hoots and hollers.

Sure, I thought. What did talent matter when you have a mob behind you?

Mercury, meanwhile, was his amenable self.

"It sounds like she's all ready to slay for some liquor!" he called out. "Am I right, ladies and gentlemen?!..."

Throughout the evening Mercury was at his muscular best: Making use of the extent of the floor, he transitioned from Russian Cossack-style low kicks to impossible crouched, scuttle walk, moving from one end of the restaurant to the other.

But despite these acts of incomparable dance, the crowd wasn't tipping either he or the other drag queens.

Pull out your billfolds! I thought.

Exasperated, I tried to set an example by extending bill after bill to the queens.

Mercury, though, (ever the professional) appeared utterly unfazed, and in response to my frequent tipping, just stopped and did a dance for me each time.

Then, in an extraordinary act of strength, Mercury (with one hand) lifted April (seated in her chair) about a foot out from the table, so to make room to perform a lap dance for her...

"When he did that lap dance on me, he actually didn't touch me, and put no weight on me at all," April commented. "He's so strong – He held himself, so there was no contact. It was just a pretend lap dance."

This despite looking as though he were seated right on top of her...

After the show Mercury stopped by our table.

"It never even crossed my mind that lap dancing was an experience I would ever have," April told him, laughing.

Seated across from me, he smiled, winked and indicated his cheek.

Hurrying from the chair I nearly fell over the table acting on the offer.

He responded with titillated shimmy of his head and shoulders...

CHAPTER TWENTY-FOUR

"Probably a lot of guys were flush with envy," April after the show of the lap dance. "Because I'm a heterosexual woman. So to cross the gender boundary – I never imagined."

Then, she smiled deviously.

"You know what I did tonight?" she said. "I intentionally put you in the aisle… I put myself in the area where the performers were not very likely to go, and I put you in a place where I knew there was dancing."

I did want to be there, though purely for artistic reasons, as I had no interest in the looks or other attention the drag queens bestowed on me.

"That's funny," April responded. "Because when I was trying to integrate the way they dance with the way I danced at Badlands, you really didn't like that. You were turned off by it. I was doing the diva way of dancing and trying to work it out of my system, and you were like, 'Ehh, I don't know my wife.' So you didn't like me acting like a drag queen."

No, I preferred the sweet, fluid dancer she was.

"He's obviously paying attention to me," she continued. "I physically wasn't in the right place, so he had to create that space. I think he did it in order to make me feel included. Or maybe give you a message. Something. It was intentional, though. Maybe it was it a message to both of us, but I'm not sure what it is?"

I thought it was his way of treating us as a package, and perhaps we'll get lucky and become friends.

"I would like that," she said. "Because I like him, too…"

CHAPTER TWENTY-FIVE

In the morning I felt the urge to watch a movie from my youth – *Frankenstein - The True Story,* starring a dazzlingly handsome Michael Sarrazin as the lovely creation for whom everything goes wrong. In this rendering of the Mary Shelley tale the creature begins his existence with all the physical beauty of youth; however, with the passage of time, he quickly reverts back to the dead flesh from which he came. And as those who made him now conspire to destroy him, like an avenging angel, he foils their every attempt, reflecting back on them the inhumanity they sought to visit upon him.

"Why are you watching that?" April asked.

I think it's because of my feelings for Mercury, I responded.

"Why would you want to compare him with Frankenstein?"

Because I'm scared.

"To the degree of Frankenstein?!"

Yeah. Here's a guy whose big and strong and beautiful, and to whom I'm attracted, and I have this fear of homosexuals.

The events surrounding this fear began innocently enough: Between my junior and senior year of college I'd been working at the Jackson Laboratories in Bar Harbor, Maine. Walking down a corridor I saw a man who appeared in some distress and asked if he was lost? He responded that he was looking for the auditorium, and I offered to take him. Along the way he asked what I was doing at the laboratory and what my aspirations were? I said I was a college student performing research and preparing to apply for medical school. He responded that he sat on the medical school admission committee at Harvard, and before that at UCLA, and if I wanted, he'd help me with my application. We agreed to meet in town, then he insisted I accompany him to his hotel room, so he could show me the personal statement he'd drafted for me.

"What are you going to do for me now that I've done this great thing for you?" he asked.

What followed was, to say the least, uncomfortable.

And, to add insult to injury, the first responses to my medical school application were rejection letters from Harvard and UCLA.

"And you think he had something to do with it?" April asked.

Yes, I said. They came months before responses from any of the other schools I applied to.

Anyway, I continued, there was nothing the least bit monstrous about Mercury. Indeed, if there's someone monstrous now, it's me. I'm no longer the possessor of the 'beauty of youth' that I was back then, with natural locks and curls in my dark brown hair. Instead, *I've* become the collection of rotting flesh – with growths under my scalp and age spots on my skin.

Yet I felt young, and was reminded of a comment an elderly patient once told me: "Being old is feeling like you're eighteen, but being stuck in an old body." That was me now.

April smiled.

"My grandmother always told me she 'feels like she's young'," she said. "She always felt that she was sixteen. I just think it's a biological instinct for young people to be attracted to youth, because, in general terms, youth will produce a healthier baby, and will have the physical stamina to deal with a baby and a toddler, and have a span of years to help raise that child through eighteen or something.

"Everyone gets old. When I look at older people, what makes them beautiful is laugh lines and disposition... You can tell someone's personality from the way their skin wrinkles. And that's beautiful. You earn those wrinkles, whichever way you get them – either by frowning or by smiling."

"And you keep your body young," she added, spiritedly. "You have a very attractive body."

"The thing I do see," she admitted sadly, "is that you are not as patient and open-hearted as you were at Rosebud. Not the 'free-flowing Dave' that you were back then. And I would so like if you got back to that softer part of yourself…"

CHAPTER TWENTY-SIX

Sitting alone in our living room in the wee hours of the morning composing a letter, a fuse in the chandelier short-circuited, sending flames along the stranded cord into the ceiling.

"Light!" I shouted, tongue-tied and terrified. "Light!"

Fortunately, by the time I coaxed April out of the bedroom, the 'fireworks' were over.

"You were saying, 'Light! Light!', and I didn't know what you meant," she scolded, good-naturedly. "I thought, 'Light'? What is he screaming about that for?' If you would have said, 'Fire!', I would've been running out of the house in a second..."

That evening we went to Lumens Lighting to get a replacement chandelier.

"I want the one shaped like a flower," April declared. "It's beautiful."

It happened that Lumens was almost directly across the street from Badlands.

"I think Mercury's hosting the drag show there tonight," April said. "Why don't we go in?..."

Inside, Mercury was dressed in street clothes and toting his suitcase.

"Hey, hey!" he called out.

When the show began, he appeared in a bright yellow banana costume.

"There's a story that goes with that," April said. "I was reading in one of his blogs that he was performing at a drag show and there was this group of evangelical protesters. So, when Mercury showed up in a yellow outfit – and with how thin he is – they asked if he had

AIDS? And called him an 'Anorexic Banana.' Since then, he's made that his calling card."

I nodded, though it seemed there was something different about him, as though he were unusually bulked up?

Then, I realized it wasn't Mercury at all, but, rather, Apple Adams dressed to look like Mercury. Indeed, not a moment later, Mercury strutted onto the stage with a necklace with the word 'APPLE' spelled in large letters, and the two announced the gag before launching into a dance number together.

"I like Apple," April commented. "She's like an earthy, strong, sixties hippy woman. She does that really well."

It happened that the other night I'd been standing next to Apple; noting his broad chested and well-developed arms, shoulders and back, it struck me that he/she had a build similar to a jackhammer operator I knew.

"Apple might be physically bigger than Mercury," April responded, "but I see her as more of a female than I see Mercury."

Nodding, I agreed – when Apple performed, she did conduct herself more 'woman' than Mercury.

But less feminine or not, I just loved the way Mercury danced – so bold and unashamed. When he put on those outfits, he was someone entirely different – someone like I wanted to be. Week after week I'd watched him enter the Capitol Garage wearing those plain clothes and sneakers, only to emerge through the curtain like Superman (albeit in heels). I envied he and the other drag queens their willingness to express themselves in ways that were fun and compelling, and had I to do all over again, I would have lived as they did – Wild and open and free.

April's face lost expression then, and she sank in the barstool.

"I don't think there's any way that could have happened for you," she responded under her breath. "I could see your dad – 'What are you doing with your life, David?' He'd never let you..."

CHAPTER TWENTY-SEVEN

At Fantastic Sams I didn't have long to wait before my hairstylist, Jasmine, was calling me back.

"Are you ready for me, Dave?" she asked, pleasantly.

Jasmine was exceedingly beautiful. If not the woman of my dreams, she was certainly the one of my visions. Just the other day the thought of her entered my head while carrying on a philosophical conversation with my friend, Sam: He asked what I thought heaven might be like? Having never considered it, I tried to sidestep the question. But when he pressed me for an answer, I turned to the side and opened my imagination – And instead of wafty clouds and pearly gates, what registered in my head was the vision of an angel that looked just like Jasmine...

"I was thinking of you," she said, applying the cape around my shoulders. "I was thinking that I hadn't seen you in a while."

I apologized, saying I'd been skiing and let my hair grow out to keep my head warm.

"Look at you," she responded, sweetly. "You're having all kinds of fun."

As though offering words of reassurance and encouragement to a small child, I thought.

Smiling, I closed my eyes to the gray-haired older man in the mirror.

She asked about my mother (who was refusing her meds in L.A.) and my father (who I'd recently visited between ski trips in Carson), then confided that she was leaving that evening for a vacation.

"So, if you'd waited one more day," she said, "I would've been out for a week."

She thanked me for the Christmas card and asked what I'd done for the holiday? Depressing the corners of my mouth, I said that I'd been attending drag shows because I'd been taken by the dancing of a particular drag queen.

"Does this person have a name?" she asked.

I told her.

"I know him," she responded. "We went to high school together, then cosmetology school. I've never been to any of his shows, but I've seen the videos he's posted... He's very humble. And very sweet. He always has been that way. Are you going to see him again?"

Yes, we had plans to see him on Saturday for my birthday.

"When exactly is your birthday?" she asked.

Tomorrow, I responded.

I looked away. Here I was about to turn fifty-five, and my effective stepmother killed herself rather than turn thirty?

Jasmine whispered to the cashier who was standing nearby.

"I'm already on it," the cashier replied.

Finishing, Jasmine announced the haircut was free.

"Our way of saying we appreciate you," she declared.

Opening my wallet, she objected when I offered her a tip.

"No, Dave," she pleaded. "It's your birthday."

But I insisted, telling her to use it on her vacation...

"Did she tell you Mercury's real name?" April asked. "Why didn't you ask her?"

Because I don't care what his name is. It didn't matter to me. He was Mercury.

"The next time you see him, you can say you know her," April added.

Yeah, I could, but what for?...

That night Jasmine came to me in a dream. We were working on a homework assignment together. She asked how I was doing? But my conduct suggested I wasn't serious about the project. She was, though...

CHAPTER TWENTY-EIGHT

What a difference a day makes? I thought, sitting up in bed.

It was the morning after my birthday celebration, and I awoke to a feeling of Mercury deep inside myself.

Physiologically, I understood what it meant: I'd let him into my endorphin system. Another way of saying, I was in love.

Puzzling over how this could be, I wracked my brains!

I saw you at the Museum,
> *And was blown away by your dancing.*
April and I met you after the show,
> *And I was taken by your friendliness.*
We followed you to the Capitol Garage,
> *And I basked in your skills as an entertainer.*
I wanted to support you,
> *Because I believed in what you're doing.*

How in the world could this happen?...

At the Capitol Garage last night April had reserved a table for four near the stage. At the last minute, though, Dino's girlfriend couldn't make it, so he came alone.

Mercury entered the diner later than usual and walked past our table looking as though in a fog.

The drag show finally started. Looking at Dino, it didn't seem like he was having much fun. I offered him a roll of dollars, but he refused.

"No!" he said, forcefully. "I'm not giving any dollar bills to guys."

He got up and went to the bar. April edged closer.

"He probably is enjoying it," she whispered. "But he's got an image to maintain…"

For the lip sync competition, when Mercury randomly selected several volunteers at the back of the restaurant, April expressed disappointment.

"All the other times he asked for birthdays," she said.

As Mercury walked past, April waved and told him it was my birthday; but instead of inviting me to join the others, he responded that he would call me up later.

"We're going to do something extra special for you," he said. "We'll put you in a special twerking contest."

I sat bolt upright, the comment having sent shivers down my spine. April, meanwhile, was nonplussed.

"Doesn't it seem to you like Mercury is having an off night?" she asked. "It seems like his energy isn't the same. He showed up late, but even then it doesn't explain why the show didn't start until 8:20? He just doesn't seem like he's in it…"

After the intermission Mercury approached us, then took me by the hand and led me up onstage. To my relief, instead of any twerking, he announced to the crowd that I'd been coming every week and supporting the drag queens and he appreciated it.

"Because we need our supporters," he declared.

Singing happy birthday, he twirled back and forth in my arms. Each time I supported him, attempting to keep him safe in his eight-inch heels, seemingly oblivious to the fact that given the amazing feats of balance he performed each night, he needed no such assistance.

At the song's end I asked if I could say a few words? Reticently, he handed me the mic.

"From childhood I've been an admirer of men in dance," I said. "This originated from the time that my mother took up ballet when I was young, and I'd peruse the dance magazines lined the bedroom and bathroom floor. I've seen Baryshnikov and other top male danseurs perform in ballet companies across the country. But, if you ask me, Mercury is the best dancer I've ever seen, and I feel so lucky I can come here and see him perform each week."

Sighs from the crowd were followed by warm applause. Indeed, the only one who didn't appear moved was Mercury.

"All right, you guys," he said. "Before anyone starts making my head swell – and I'm not talking about the one on top of my shoulders – I just have to say that Hellen [the other drag queen performing that evening] is the dancer. I think of myself as more a model."

I nodded.

I suppose that makes sense given how tall he is, I conceded, returning to my chair...

After the show Mercury passed our table, and April asked if he had plans for the night?

"I'm doing my usual," he demurred. "Going for something at Jack-in-the-Box."

"Well, come out with us sometime then," I interjected. "We'll take you to someplace other than Jack-in-the-Box."

"No," he insisted. "I usually hibernate during the winter. I hate going out in the cold. Maybe when it warms up…"

Staying for karaoke, Dino and April got onstage and sang The Beatle's *Birthday* song.

They say it's your birthday
We're gonna have a good time.

Later, essentially the whole of the restaurant staff (waiter, bartender, DJ) joined Dino and I for Joe Cocker's *With a Little Help from My Friends*.

At the end of the night I slipped the DJ a twenty. But he didn't want to take it and tried putting it back in my pocket...

"Dave, that was worth so much more than twenty bucks," April commented. "That was like having a karaoke room to ourselves for hours with our own personal DJ…"

CHAPTER TWENTY-NINE

Entering April's room where she'd been sleeping with Sweetness, she chided me for looking sleepy.

"You're probably not used to being out late," she declared, smiling. "Party boy! Those drag queens are a bad influence on you. Probably when you were younger – even in your twenties – your dad said something like that to you: 'Oh, these people are a bad influence', and you were like, 'I'm not going to do that – I'm going to be a doctor', right? Goody two shoes."

Nodding, I kept silent, till finally sharing the feeling I awoke to.

"But he brushed you off when you invited him to do something!" she responded. "If I was interested in somebody – and I'm pretty shy – I would create situations to go and do something."

I agreed, though I still felt a lingering doubt: There was the ease I experienced standing next to him onstage – The tenderness I felt towards him – And now this?

"Because he's cute!" she insisted. "He's sweet. And he's a great dancer. And he looks you right in the eye and he touches you. And you're starved for touch."

She sighed.

"You enjoy watching him dance," she began, "but would you have any sexual feelings for him if he was someplace like Chippendales?... What I mean is, he's a fish wearing the colors of a different kind a fish. And you are attracted to the colors, even though it's a male fish wearing female fish colors. Because you're designed to be attracted to the female colors. But they're on a male fish, so you're still attracted to the female colors, but you're having trouble because they're on a male."

I shook my head. Though I'd never experienced feelings like this for a man before, I still wasn't convinced they were sexual. It was confusing, though – How did this happen?

"Because he was touching you," she insisted. "He said, 'I love you.' It was part of the show."

"So you got seduced," she asserted. "Yes. You got attracted. You got snared. Mercury Rising is definitely a huntress. She wouldn't dance the way she dances – to break all autonomous boundaries – if she weren't seducing – if she weren't hunting."

Why refer to it as 'hunting'? He was simply performing.

"Well, he's performing an active hunt," she responded. "He has not taken you up on your invitation. I invited him the first time I saw him. You've invited him last night? So, he hasn't taken us up on any of our openings. So I'm not sure at all if he is hunting. But he is definitely acting out hunting. He is acting out an available female, who is very, very available."

But could it be that there was some real energy of intention that I was connecting with?

"I don't know him well enough to know," she replied. "But we both heard him live and on tape saying that he loves attention. In that interview he presented himself saying he didn't set out to do drag. It was a happenstance that he got feminized on a drunken dare at a gay bar, and he got attention, and he loved the attention, so he was like, 'I want to do more of that.' So he's saying his motivation is attention."

Well, he sure got my attention.

"He got my attention, too!" she exclaimed. "I'm the one who said, 'Hey, Dave, you got to come see this', right? And I'm the one who said, 'Hey, let's go to his show.' But does he want more than people simply enjoying watching him dance and feminized himself? Does he want the extra step of a relationship with the fans?"

"I am also attracted to his androgyny," she admitted. "But in a much more mild way – not like you. Because I also know that, for me, well… If you turn gay, you can maybe have a relationship with him. I can't do anything whatsoever to have a relationship with him. For me, there is no path for him to be attracted to me. Unless he's bi. And anyways, I'm twice his age and also fat."

And I'm even older. Though I contended that if April still regarded me as attractive, anyone could.

"But we have been together so long," she responded. "I know for myself that I'm capable of finding someone attractive just based on history – and love.

"So I can't say if he finds you attractive. He hasn't singled you out… He has singled you out as a super-fan, but he hasn't singled you out in any other way. The things he's done with you could suggest that he's interested, but he does that with so many other people. I do perceive a difference in degree of how he interacts with you compared to other people, but I don't know."

"It's the ultimate crush," she concluded. "The unattainable object…"

CHAPTER THIRTY

I'd made plans to ski that day with my friend, Sam. On the way to the resort I stayed mostly quiet, still puzzling over the feelings I awoke to. Once on the slopes, though, it didn't take long for me to lose myself in skiing – especially with Sam there, whose skiing was simply magical, like beholding a 'Ski Sensei' right out of the pages of Richard Bach's *Illusions.*

Then, on the way home, Sam asked about last night's show?

"Are you're still enjoying Mercury's performances?" he asked. "Was there something new that Mercury was doing? The way he was moving? The act?"

No, I responded, reserved. It was basically the same. It just came down to he and the other drag queens being great dancers. I just admired these men for so bringing out their feminine side in dancing.

"Right," he said. "Well, when they do it so well, it's art, isn't it?"

It's beautiful is what it is, I thought.

"Even when I see a wonderfully styled car," he continued, "or a piece of work – a sculpture or something – it really brings out something that's deep within us. It just strikes the mind and releases chemicals that make us feel joy."

Nodding, I shared about Mercury bringing me up onstage and then my expressing my admiration for him.

"You recognize talent," Sam commented. "I'm not surprised the crowd responded to you the way it did. You are a professional speaker, Dave. You give book talks. You give talks about opioids. You give pain management talks. And for all of them you've gotten great reviews. So I can understand this."

But Mercury didn't seem to understand: He told the crowd he was just another dancer and didn't seem to grasp how special he is.

"Well, you have to remember, in his line it's very competitive," Sam responded. "I'm no expert in transgender, but the transgender people I know have been fighting for their identity for so long that they're kind of sensitive. So you have to be very careful of even praising somebody in a group - unless you spread out the praise.

"Mercury has to live with all these people, so to speak. And if it leaks out that he is a prima donna or something, I think people of this group are quite sensitive.

"I know I just had to be with kid gloves all the time when I was with this crowd, and my hands got slapped a few times. The first time I will went to a drag show was in San Francisco on Broadway. And I had a great time. 'These people are so talented,' I thought. That's what I really enjoyed. Just talent. Doesn't matter what it is, really. As long as it's done with talent and in good taste.

"So I'm glad you're having a good time. You appreciate it and that's the most important thing. And you're not attached to stigmas, which a lot of people are. It's like somebody does a fantastic drawing or a painting, but then you study about the artist, and maybe you don't approve of their political viewpoint, or they're disfigured, and it turns you off, and all of a sudden, you don't see their art the same way, because now you've got this bias – this prejudice. And there are a lot of people who are like that. But you're not that way, Dave, and that's the wonderful thing about you. You appreciate things for what they are, and you're not influenced by heady biases. I think that's one of the things that makes you a really great person. You're very, very open. I wish more people were like that. I think the world would be a better place."

I shook my head and finally confided the feelings I awoke to.

"The night before I declared that I was there for his talent," I lamented. "But these feelings suggest something else."

"Dave, your love is love beyond the sexual," Sam replied, reassuringly. "I think it could be part of it – I'm not going to say it's not – but loving someone is a very complex thing, and it's a strong emotional thing. So it can be complex.

"And I know you. You're a very deep person. That's the reason why you're a writer. This is why you became at doctor. This is why you went for a PhD. You look for more complexities in a relationship than what other people do. And that's a good thing, if you ask me, because in that complexity – eventually with time – you will realize and work things out and arrive at a more realistic picture.

"And that's not a bad thing. That's what love at first site is. That's what attracts us. That's what makes people take on these really incredible endurance tests. That's what makes them conquer Antarctica. If a person really did study it too much, they probably wouldn't do it, because they'd say, 'I could get frostbite. I can lose my toes. I could lose my nose. My ears.' All of a sudden, you go, 'You know what? I'm not gonna do it.'

"But people don't think that. They just think of all the wonderful things, and the adrenaline they have, and, 'It's can be so cool', and, 'I'll really see how strong I really am', and say, 'Okay, I'm going to go for it. And no one's gonna stop me.'

"And we got all these flaws – or else we'd just do everything perfect. And then we wouldn't learn anything. So imperfection makes us perfect, so to speak."

He laughed.

"So enjoy it while you can. And turn over the cards to complete the pieces of the picture. Just give yourself time. You'll see it all in time.

"It's kind of nice to feel things. And it has nothing to do with one gender over another. It's all about human beings. It's only society that put us in a thing of genders and such. But, as you develop, you'll understand what your preference really is.

"So explore the edges a little bit. Walk on the wild side. You'll pull yourself back to who you really are deep down. You'll say, 'I really don't like guys, but I appreciate what he has that I don't have. And that's why I like him. Because he is the type of person physically that I would like to be or has these capabilities that I'd like.' So that it's less of loving someone than wishing you were them. Again, it's complex. I think whenever you feel certain things, I would let them incubate for a while."

"Throughout my life, Dave, I've had idols," he confided. "Guys who I would like to be like. The guy who was popular with all the girls – I thought, 'I want to be like him.' And I get close, and then I'm able to do these things, and I achieve this goal, and I thank them, and then I move on to another idol.

"Other times, love relationships are like that: You grow with them, and then you move on, so you can keep getting better..."

CHAPTER THIRTY-ONE

"The thing that has me confused about Dave's attraction to Mercury," April told Carl, "is he doesn't like when I wear make-up. Which I don't really care about, since I don't wear make-up – So it fits my personality. And I wouldn't wear dresses like Mercury, either. And I wouldn't dance so suggestively like Mercury does. So it's just all interesting to me. And I was pointing that out to him that I think that if a woman would do the things that Mercury does, then he wouldn't really think very highly of her. But on Mercury, he likes it."

"But there is androgyny involved, so it's more complicated," Carl said. "It's not a woman. It's something in between."

"It's completely different," he continued. "Something absolutely fascinating, because it's a category that serves as a bridge to somewhere in between."

"Dave, let me ask you this," he inserted. "If you saw a Mercury dressed in jeans and a casual outfit, would you be attracted to him?"

Probably not, I responded.

"And that's my assumption," Carl asserted. "That you love the androgyny of it. You love the in between-ness of the whole thing, and it's just fascinating to you.

"And that's why there's a lot of violence around drag. Because it falls in that area of being permissive with some people who are really closeted and misogynistic. Who will fall for these women, and then try to negotiate some sort of relationship outside of a drag show or bar, and they become corporal relationships... Because you'll have these straight men who are terribly attracted, but, then, after a sexual encounter, they feel all of this self-loathing and anger towards the person who has made them go with the same sex. That's why a lot of these transsexuals get beaten up afterwards. Because the straight partner can't believe what he's just done…"

CHAPTER THIRTY-TWO

Carl was right – When I'd told April about my feelings and she'd reminded me that Mercury had blown me off about taking him out, I had experienced a flash of anger.

"I said 'brushed' you off," April asserted. "'Blew' you off means something different entirely – especially in his circle."

"But you felt angry because of the rejection, right?" Carl asked. "Still, it's great that you're open to all these feelings and you're not repressing at all."

I certainly wasn't repressing anything. Indeed, the other night I'd dreamt I was in a summer camp contest and tasked with completing three projects in order to win a prize. Each of the projects had to be completed within a certain amount of time. One of them was making a drawing. Finishing the sketch I asked for a scissors to cut it out, then set about the other two tasks. In the end I received a total score of 13 – just enough to beat out the next highest scoring competitor. But ascending the winner's podium, a judge intervened.

"Well, I didn't want to do this," she began, "but so-and-so is the winner, because I'm disqualifying Dr. Fischer two points for being late with his picture."

In response, I stomped my feet.

"That isn't fair!" I objected. "I didn't finish drawing the picture late! I just cut it out from the larger sheet of paper!"

And despite an inner voice telling me to just go along and not make a fuss (as would be my usual pattern), I refused...

"Again, you're getting to know more about yourself through this experience," Carl affirmed.

Yes, but I was making efforts to distance myself, as well. For this week's show I reserved a table in the back because I didn't want the looks and touches if they weren't real.

"But Mercury is a performer," Carl insisted. "And as a performer, all of the genders are blended. And that's what makes it exciting – that it's a blend of everything."

But if it's an act, I don't want it. If there's one thing I can't stomach, it's deceit in any form.

"Wait a minute," Carl interrupted. "You're interacting with a performer while he is performing. And yet you don't want it to be a performance? You want Mercury to be really meaning it during the performance?"

Yeah, I responded. I feel lied to.

"I have to say, I think you're setting yourself up," he said.

April nodded in agreement.

"You are putting yourself upfront where the performer is performing," Carl continued, "and yet you are asking for very real emotions to be behind the performer's performance."

"That's part of his spiel," April added. "To be seductive. To have charisma. In the show he plays a seductive woman – an expressive, liberated, seductive woman. And he does it to everybody. Maybe it's because you're feeling something that you only see him doing it to you. I see him do to other people the same thing that he does to you. And you could see it, too – If you were looking at him with clear eyes. You could see that a moment after he does it to you, he does it to somebody else.

"What I saw was that he touched your hand and mouthed the words in the song, 'I love you', and then he went on, and I saw him do the same thing to someone else. The song came around to that same sentence, and he did that same thing with somebody else."

I nodded, downtrodden.

Performance, I uttered.

"I'm sure he likes you," April responded. "As a performer would like a fan."

"And he's probably leery," she added. "It's very possible that the reason he has not pursued a personal interaction with you aside from the shows is because he's leery of all these things."

Yeah, he should be. Who in the world would want to be in a relationship that isn't 'consummated'? Doesn't offer that possibility?

Then, I recalled my beloved friend, Ethel, who I took care of when she had cancer. It didn't matter that our relationship wasn't consummated. I didn't even want that – Because I loved her so much and was afraid if it became sexual, it would detract from my ability to care for her.

And it was trying to find that 'consummation' in someone who looked like Ethel that led me to Timina; whose lies broke me, so that I didn't feel I could trust anyone; and went searching for April, who I could trust.

"I hope this is helping you with categorizing lie versus truth," Carl commented. "Because here it's really true, even though in many ways it's an illusion."

"I don't see Mercury as a liar," April said. "I see him as a person who is exploring femininity as a man. And I see him as somebody exploring seductiveness. But I think that he is honest in that he does it in the show, and he has not taken you up on your invitation to meet him and get to know him outside the show."

"But I don't want to contradict, Dave," she said tenderly. "He has to figure this out for himself. It's not my place to figure this out for him.

"On the one hand, he says he isn't interested. On the other, his whole body language says something else. I am feeling he is infatuated."

"Dave's the only one who can figure this out," Carl asserted. "And these things play as they play out. Who knows? And as long as everybody is OK with it, it's fine."

Turning to April, I asked if she was OK with it?

"I am and I'm not," she responded. "You are my husband, and there is the element of, 'My husband's having a crush on a drag queen', and being like, 'I can't believe this is happening...'"

CHAPTER THIRTY-THREE

"I am finding it interesting," April continued. "Because one of the things that I've been thinking about is that, watching the shows, I'm getting to see a male's point of view on femininity."

"I think it's playing with female stereotypes," Carl said. "And it's exaggerating them. And it's perhaps again trying to find the essence in exaggeration. Trying to find the essence in almost farce."

"But when I watch these guys," April said, "it's almost like they're doing women more than I am. They can do makeup way better than I can."

"Yeah, but they teach each other," Carl said. "They are artists at makeup."

"And they move in a feminine way that even I can't do," April said. "So I look at it, and it's a version of female that even I don't get to."

"I have a gay friend who does an imitation of macho straight man," Carl said. "And he is absolutely hilarious, because everything is spitting on the floor, and using a really deep voice – 'I'm going out hunting! Where's my gun?!' It's such an exaggeration, so that it's almost like he's doing drag in the reverse."

"He's a drag king!" April and I declared in unison.

"So these things are absolute exaggerations," Carl continued, "and I don't know many straight men who would fit the stereotype, or even want it."

"That's why I say it's all very interesting," April responded. "I've always been drawn to drag shows, but Dave hasn't. Like we would be in a gay bar, and the drag show would come up, and I was drawn to it, and Dave would always be wanting to leave."

73

"And I frankly never have," Carl asserted. "Because I'm attracted to guys. I'm on the other end of the spectrum."

I thought I was attracted to androgyny because I want to connect with my feminine side. Particularly in dance, where I love the feeling of flowing with the music and merging strength with grace.

And that's what Mercury is capable of – more than anyone I've ever seen. That's why, after a lifetime of turning away from drag shows, Mercury comes along and it felt like being hit by a truck!

"And I'm also attracted to androgyny," April said. "Not because I see myself as androgynous – I'm more of a hippie girl – but because of the whole thought of switching roles."

"And that's something the two of you have in common," Carl inserted. "It's a liminal place... Something in between – where all change takes place, because it's neither one thing or the other. A suspension of possibilities where healing can happen. It's in this magical area – where things fall out of the ordinary and into the creative – the possible – the pure potentiality. It's a very fertile area..."

CHAPTER THIRTY-FOUR

Renatta was a rehab specialist who I worked with at the Winter Sanctuary (an industrial warehouse converted into a 200-bed shelter where a number of my homeless patients were housed). As she was the one who owned the red Camaro (My car was a twenty-five year old Honda), she did the driving. Looking at her, it struck me that she was the kind of woman most of these drag queens patterned themselves after: Big hair, beautiful features, lots of make-up, bawdy, she was easily the envy of any of these men...

"Did you have a birthday recently?" she asked.

Yes, I responded. It was last week.

"What did you do for it?"

I went and saw Mercury.

"How was that?"

The dancing was OK, though even Mercury posted an apology after the show, saying he was sick and that's why he hadn't performed to his usual standards. Then, I told her about his 'brushing' me off.

"Did you feel rejected?" she asked.

Yeah, I admitted.

"Don't!" she responded. "It could've been that after performing, he really was tired. It takes a lot of energy to prepare and put on that make up and then perform, so that at the end of the night they're really wiped out."

"I've read that a lot of these guys suffer from depression," she continued. "Like a really high number – like ninety percent. So that, on the stage, they're happy and exuberant and bursting with energy. But outside of their stage character, they're really somebody else..."

CHAPTER THIRTY-FIVE

As I'd requested, the next Saturday April and I were seated at a table near the back of the diner, so to dial back the experience with Mercury.

"Because you're not as much a part of the performance?" April asked.

Yes, I responded.

She smiled.

"I think a joke he made was pertinent to you," she commented. "The one when he said, 'Have one drink, and then another, and then a third, and by that time you'll think I am really a woman.' I think he was saying that because you're not the only one to get it confused..."

The most memorable event of the evening was a rendering of the Sonny and Cher collaboration *Bang Bang* by a drag queen named Luna Nova.

Bang bang, he shot me down
Bang bang, I hit the ground
Bang bang, that awful sound
Bang bang, my baby shot me down

Performed with depth and sensitivity, honesty and intimacy, Luna's performance reached to the core of me.

And because of her gender fluidity, her message went beyond a call against violence against women; but a stand against intolerance and acts of persecution perpetrated against any vulnerable person or population...

At the song's end Luna put a hand to her heart and red fluid oozed from the bosom of her gown. The lights dimmed and she departed. But some of the artificial blood had spilled to the ground, and Mercury came out with a towel and feverishly scrubbed the stage floor on his hands and knees.

"Bitch!" he uttered under his breath, comically, to the relief of myself and perhaps others in the crowd who who'd been similarly affected, and now chuckled quietly and breathed a sigh of relief...

CHAPTER THIRTY-SIX

Mercury had sported a green wig during the show that was now being passed around by the members of the audience taking selfies with him.

"Dave, I think you'd look good in that wig," April said. "Let's take a picture with you in it."

April put the wig on me, then Mercury came and adjusted it before posing with me for a photo.

"I wanted to take the picture with it because I thought the green wig would work for Dave," April told Mercury.

"I think he would look better in a blue wig," he responded. "Electric blue."

Mercury had worn a such a wig for a particularly introspective and sensual number he'd performed to Yaeji's *Raingurl.*

Mother Russia in my cup
And my glasses foggin' up
Make it rain girl, make it rain

"I thought your version was better than the official video," I told him.

"Well, that's saying a lot," he responded, hugging me. "Thank you..."

"He did give us lots of hugs," April commented later. "When I hug him, he often doesn't have clothes there, so I was touching the skin of a guy, and for me its ingrained response to feel like it's too forward on my part, so in the beginning it freaked me out. Now, I've gotten more used to it."

"In the show, he doesn't have a lot of personal boundaries," she added. "He not just lets but invites people into his personal space -

and to touch. And he touches. And normally strangers don't cross that physical boundary."

I love that he lets people in that way, I replied.

Then, it struck me that I'd never shared anything like this with him. Here I was someone who prided himself on 'telling more truths faster', yet everywhere I was withholding my thoughts and feelings?

"You have said it, Dave," April insisted. "'The love'... That was sort of in the beginning of going here – the first or second time."

"In some ways it might be good to keep on having this energy," she added. "This fantasy energy for the unattainable..."

CHAPTER THIRTY-SEVEN

Was I in this 'fantasy' to avoid psychic pain? I wondered. My medical assistant was recovering from a near fatal traumatic head injury and rather than being a bigger part of his recovery, I was going to drag shows. The same was true of my mother.

"But your medical assistant isn't up for evening stuff," April responded. "You asked him to join us, and he said he thought the music would be too loud and give him headaches."

"Your mom is a whole other kettle of fish," she continued. "You would be totally visiting your mom all the time if she was halfway welcoming or even tolerable. The reason you're not there is because she closed the door."

I flashed to our last visit - the way she kicked us out of the house.

"And it's the same for your brother," April added. "You're not welcome there either."

Still, it seemed to me the reason I wasn't frequenting my mother's was because the life and relationships there left me mostly dis-inspired – like the way I didn't want to live...

That evening at Sidetrax Mercury walked out onstage in brunette, bouffant hairstyle wig, lip syncing to Queen's *I Want to Break Free.* With a broom in hand, he brushed furiously at the floor as though sweeping away the vestiges of an unwanted life.

Then, dancing into the crowd, he gripped my outstretched hand, and (leaving the bills in place) twirled back-and-forth in my arms...

CHAPTER THIRTY-EIGHT

At the next week's show April and I were seated next to four handsome gay men – their shirts mostly unbuttoned to reveal shapely, muscular chests.

"I find them attractive," April commented. "Do you find them attractive?"

Yes, I responded. They're attractive men.

"Are you sexually attracted to them the way you are to Mercury?"

No, I said.

"Why?" she asked. "They might not be wearing female clothing, but, to me, they're on the same branch as Mercury."

There was more than just looks and sexual orientation when it came to Mercury. There was a whole sequence of events that influenced my feelings for him.

As for the men at the other table, I didn't know them – save the thought that to be as 'out' as they were, they had to be pretty tough.

"And you don't think Mercury has had to be tough?" she asked.

I do. And I've seen it. That's among the reasons I was taken so off-guard that first night we met him, and he greeted us with smiles and laughter.

"But how much do you think that's his persona?" she asked. "And how much do you think it's him?"

I didn't know. And maybe Mercury and these men were birds of the 'same branch', but, given the choice, I preferred to keep my distance.

"They're intimidating to you?" she asked.

As she knew well from my Harvard Professor experience, my interactions with gay men had not always been the most pleasant.

"But if they wouldn't 'peck' at you, would you be sexually attracted?" she asked.

No, I said, emphatically. I'm attracted to girls.

"That's what I'm questioning," she said. "How is Mercury a 'girl'? What's feminine about him?"

Everything! I responded, exasperated. He's warm and gentle. Soft and tender. Beautiful.

Then I recalled something a girlfriend from medical school told me.

"What makes you so attractive is that you're so soft, but, at the same time, so undeniably male."

And for the first time it struck me that my feeling for Mercury might be less something sexual than an unconscious attempt to get back to a less hardened version of myself...

CHAPTER THIRTY-NINE

Surfing the Web, April read news of historic flooding around Vegas.

"Some places have been swept away," she said. "You better call you friend, Ben, and make sure he's alright."

It was against my better judgment, as it was the time of day that Ben slept before his midnight shift.

"But he might get up and unknowingly drive to work, and be swept up in some rising water somewhere," April responded.

Showing me photos of the devastation, I decided to call and wound up leaving a message. To my surprise, it wasn't long before I received a text back.

Dave this is Michele,
Please note that Bens schedule for work from 1 am to 3pm.
Ben is sleeping by 5:30 PM in order to get 7 hours sleep.
I ask you to please be respectful of his time constraints and need for sleep.
Thank you for understanding my protection of him.

I began to compose an apology, then stopped.

Bitch, I thought. He could have had a life in dance had it not been for her. He gave it all away.

Another text appeared.

Hi, Michele again here,
I listened to your message and thank you for your concern.
Ben and I and our house is fine.
Much love...

I began to write, but again desisted.

I would have been a better partner to him than her, I thought. I would have helped him achieve his dreams. I wouldn't have held him back. I would have let him shine and given him that beautiful life he was capable of...

CHAPTER FORTY

Ben called the next morning. Apologizing for the text from Michele, he laughed, referring to her as his 'Mama bear', just looking out for him.

"So, how have you been doing, Dave?" he asked.

I told him about Mercury, saying that his performing was head and shoulders above anything I'd ever seen in drag.

"Most people don't get that entertainment is an expression of your spirit," he responded. "Many people bury their spirit when they perform. For them, their source is from hating life. Their negative. You can sense it. You sense when an entertainer has a love for life. Or when they have a hate for life. You can see it in a shallow performance. When there are leeches out there on stage, just trying to suck up The energy. Or when they are givers.

"In the drag world, it's about fun. But people make it about being sexy first, instead of fun first. That's probably why you like Mercury. Because he shares his spirit. He's spirit first. He shares his zest for life. And makes it magical.

"Everybody believes in the Freudian theory that everything is about sex. But it's not. It's about spirit.

"You connect with him spiritually. You connect with his spirit. His spirit awakens your spirit. Your spirit supports his spirit. In a positive way. And you connect. And there's nothing sinister or wrong about that. You're not supposed to shut that off. We're told to shut it off, but you're not supposed to. You're supposed to understand it,. It's not about anything you gain; It's about spirits intermingling freely. You get his spirit. He gets yours. It's like, yeah, you can connect that way. It's just that most people don't. They don't understand it, and they take it is something animalistic, Because they take it as something physical instead of something spiritual. So they go down, 'Well, I guess I'm attracted to that person physically.' But you don't have to be physically attracted to someone to be attracted to them. You're attracted to them because your spirits are connected.

"There's not too many spirits you can connect with out there. Most spirits help walls up. Most spirits you don't want to connect with, Because when you do, there's too much pain there. Or their spirits aren't free.

"You have always had this compassionate spirit in you. You like seeing light. You connect with good spirits. You've gone through times in your life when you close touch with that at times, but your spirit is light. It's love. It's compassion. And love and compassion is what transforms life. That's would begets new life. It also gets you lots of pain because in birthing life, there's always pain. Which is probably why people don't go there. In order to be compassionate, you've got to feel pain. Like when you're a kid, and you have achy muscles, and your mom says, "that's just growing pains." going through pains because your body is transforming. It's converting things into a new form.

"So don't worry about your connection. Embrace it. Know your light, and support his.

"That's why people entertain. At least, that's why the real good ones entertain. It's not to get admiration. They perform to show their spirit and uplift people. They're sending their spirit out into the room, And spreading what they know about healing. I'm sure that when he's on stage it's about uplifting you and freeing your spirit. Break the boundaries that you put on it. So it sounds like a great thing."

I talked about Ethel, and the fact that even though I was crazy attracted to the woman, I made an effort to keep out the physical, because it was so important to me to care for her above anything else.

"Well, you learned one of the secrets of love. That love can go far beyond the physical. Just seeing someone beautiful, and wanting to have sex with them, belittles it. Belittles your attraction. Makes it smaller, And less important. And drive a wedge between your connection. Even if you don't voice it, your spirits know . No the difference between someone who loves their spirit and unconditionally supports it. Don't need to get anything from it in order to support it. And that's a pure sense of love. You don't have to get anything from them in order to love them…"

CHAPTER FORTY-ONE

Getting off the phone with Ben, I went to April's room.

"Sorry I was on the phone with Mercury so long," I said.

In turn, April laughed hysterically: In a first order Freudian slip, I'd thoroughly outed myself, essentially confessing deeper feelings for my childhood friend than I knew – just as she'd suspected.

"You had a little crush on him I suppose when you were growing up," she said.

I nodded.

Of course I did…

CHAPTER FORTY-TWO

Driving to the drag show, April read Mercury's most recent blogpost.

"He says he went to the doctor and got diagnosed with a broken rib," April said. "Isn't that something that needs to be in a cast?"

You couldn't cast a broken rib, I responded. The ribs are involved in breathing, so they can't be immobilized that way.

"Can dancing put him at any risk?" she asked.

He would probably be all right as long as he didn't overdo it.

"What could happened to him if he does?"

The worst thing was if the fractured rib got displaced and tore the fabric of the lung causing it to collapse.

Then, I flashed to the first patient I saw die in front of me. He had AIDS and tuberculosis. I was standing right outside his hospital room when I witnessed him bolt threw the door holding his neck and collapsed in front of me.

I initiated CPR, but couldn't get adequate chest compressions.

"Something's wrong," I told the medical residents who'd responded to the code and were now all around me. "I'm not able to compress his chest."

"Move off," one told me.

But their chest compressions weren't moving the chest any more than mine, and they were pushing so hard that the patient's skin was being pulled away from him sternum.

"No!" I cried. "You're not compressing his chest! It's not moving!"

I felt for a pulse at the patient's carotid artery, but there wasn't any.

"There's no pulse!" I exclaimed. "Your chest compressions are ineffective!"

More residents dove in, and I was totally displaced, till all I could do was hover around and helplessly watch.

When the code was called, I escorted the patient's lifeless body to the morgue. Having performed a fellowship in Pathology, I was familiar with the Pathologist who was tasked with performing the autopsy.

"What happened, Dave?" the Pathologist asked.

I told him.

"Dave, please get a 50 mL syringe, fill it halfway with water, insert a needle, then bring it to me," he said.

I did as he asked. Handing the water-filled syringe to the pathologist, he thrust the needle through the patient's chest wall. Then, withdrawing back on the plunger, bubbles of air percolated through the water layer into the shaft...

"So if you would have done that during the code," April said, "the patient would have lived?"

Yes, it was a totally preventable death.

"So instead of pressing on him, you were supposed to take out the air," she said. "And they were just giving him more air."

Yes, they were just going through the motions, instead of really evaluating and looking to understand.

In turn, they sealed his fate - Killing him.

"And they were a couple of years older, so you couldn't tell them what to do?"

Yes, they were the residents, and I was the lowly medical student who didn't know anything.

"So they had the MD behind their name, and you didn't," she said. "Did you see it on their faces that they knew what they did?"

They didn't know, and I don't think they cared. It was a general hospital, in which life was cheap, and, for most in training, the patients there amounted to little more than a source of practice.

"All these scum-bag patients you come in contact with while you're doing your training," an upper level resident told me while I was a medical student, "you have to figure, 'They don't matter.' What matters is you're at the top of the ladder. By the time you get to the level of training we're at, you're on the superior rung of society..."

"Well, maybe you ought to tell him," April said, referring to Mercury and the potential complications of his rib fracture.

He'll be OK, I responded. Just as long as he isn't too physical, and isn't throwing himself to the ground. He knows how to protect himself...

But I was wrong, as he did perform the death drops that evening.

And there was something else I noticed – that despite all the gaiety and high spiritedness in his way of speaking, there was a certain laser focus to him that I could see it in his eyes – as though when he performed, his eyes displayed a lack of expression, so as to almost appear shark-like in their intensity...

"He said in a blog after the show that even with the broken rib, when he does those death drops, he doesn't experience pain during the performance," April commented. "He says it's because there's so much adrenaline pumping through him..."

CHAPTER FORTY-THREE

Skating with Sam at The Rink I described Mercury's death drops in spite of the broken rib.

"Patients have told me that broken ribs hurt like hell," I commented. "How was he able to tolerate that kind of pain?"

"It is amazing how the mind works," Sam responded. "There's the emotion of thrill, and to be a performer, and to impress people, and to do what you're supposed to be doing up on stage before the crowd. And the problem is, Are you doing it for yourself, or are you doing it for the crowd? Because there is a really fine and dangerous line there. Because if you play to the crowd too much, caution gets tossed to the wind, and you would do almost anything to please the crowd."

"I've seen this happen," he continued. "It could be a good thing when it pushes people to improve. But when it takes them beyond their capabilities, yes, it's very dangerous."

But what was beyond Mercury's capabilities? I thought. And what does it say about me that I'm watching this guy essentially dancing on a tightrope without a net underneath him, and I'm inspired by that?

"It's pushing you to make yourself better," Sam replied, "and you enjoy that. And there's nothing wrong with that. You push yourself very hard, but you do it in a very good manner. You make your mistakes every once in a while when you push a little bit too hard, but then you back off. You get injured, but then you do recover.

"So when it comes to pushing yourself, you're not in the middle, but you're also not in that third deviation – like you're extreme. You're more in the second deviation, and that's a good place to be, because it makes you better, but it does it in a more cautious and moderate manner.

"Whereas Mercury lives right on the edge. And that's a dangerous place. Because if things aren't just exactly right, and you're off a little bit that day – Boom! – you're on the wrong side of the fence."

"You just hope this isn't an addiction," he concluded, "and he doesn't lose his way..."

CHAPTER FORTY-FOUR

The Capitol Garage expanded their karaoke to include Thursday nights. Among those who sang that evening was an attractive person who did Alanis Morissette's *You Oughta Know.* Wearing boyish clothes (baseball jacket, baseball cap, workman's boots), her frame was slight yet masculine (with wide shoulders and narrow hips), but her voice was feminine and cried out with feeling...

"I bought her a drink," April said.

Because you liked her singing? I inquired.

"Yeah," she responded. "But I'd never bought anyone a drink, and didn't quite know how to go about it, and was a little hesitant. Then I saw her go up to the bar and order a drink, so I went over there, and put down a $10 bill, and I was like, 'I'd like to pay for this. I really enjoyed your singing. I'd like to pay for your drink', and she accepted. She actually appreciated it, because she told me she does something else for her day job, but puts a lot of work in her music."

"But you thought she was a man?" April added. "But after she started singing, did you realize she was a woman?"

Citing her wide shoulders and prominent hand veins, I said I thought she was a man transitioning.

"But she has such a voice of a woman," she responded.

Likely from taking estrogen, I said.

April turned.

"With Mercury I never see him as a woman," she confided. "I always see him as a man. And with her, I saw her as a woman."

Yes, though none of that seemed to matter.

"She sang beautifully," I said...

CHAPTER FORTY-FIVE

April told Carl my karaoke was improving.

"He's more animated," she said. "He was more engaged. And he was singing louder, with his full voice."

Not only that, I was singing well beyond my usual range, as though between weeks I was making these wide quantum leaps in ability.

"It's expanding your feeling about things," Carl commented. "But I'm not sure what you're leaping to?"

I thought it was about being more free.

"And I'm also being more free," April inserted. "I was almost thinking of writing to Mercury... Telling him about how coming to see him all these weeks has catalyzed this process of me and Dave letting go and being freer and being ourselves."

"I'm sure Mercury could get what you're saying," Carl responded. "Because I think – as 'Mercury' – he experiences great freedom."

But I wondered how much I could tell Mercury? The other night when I told him I'd enjoyed the show, he demurred, referring to it as a 'good distraction' – when for me it was anything but that, and more and more I was living for Mercury's performing and counting the days till Saturday.

"I think it's great if it makes you happy," Carl commented. "But to be in each moment – appreciating the potential of each moment – is more what life's about."

"And in all this," April added, "he's barricading himself at a window table in the middle of the restaurant where Mercury can't get that close."

"Why are you doing that?" Carl asked.

"Because Mercury interacts with the crowd," April inserted. "And he's very sensual. He'll hold your hand. He'll give you very direct eye contact. He'll look right at you as he's mouthing the words from the song. And I think he really got to Dave, especially when he mouthed the words 'I love you.' But I saw him do the same thing just someone else at the next point in that song. He mouthed the same thing to another person."

"So, it wasn't specifically directed to Dave from your observation?" Carl asked.

"Well, he wasn't the only one," April responded. "But it was really getting to Dave. He was really getting seduced. And I think when Dave understood that it wasn't just him – that it was Mercury's performance – he decided he wanted off of the hot seat."

"It fascinates me your feelings about this guy, Dave," Carl said. "It also fascinates me that you're living for Saturday nights. Because the work you're doing is so important. And the work really excited you a lot. And it sounds like it's not exciting you to the same extent now..."

CHAPTER FORTY-SIX

At the clinic a homeless patient came saying he'd been really depressed lately and that's why he'd recently tested positive for high levels of meth in his system.

"The reason," he explained, "is because my wife died."

I sat bolt upright: I'd met this woman only a month before. She was young and vital.

"Yeah, I know," he responded. "She fell at our camp by the river... She was just getting some water. But it was night time, and it was dark, so she stumbled on a rock and fell back. By the time we got her to the hospital, she wound up dying. I keep blaming myself and feel really bad.

"In the meanwhile..."

"Can I have some Viagra?" April inserted.

I nodded.

Yes, I replied. He said he'd met a new woman and didn't want anything to 'get in the way.'

At issue was his Meth use, which combined with Viagra could lead to stroke, of which he'd already had two.

"I haven't used Meth in a week," he'd said. *"I'm not gonna use it again..."*

"Do you think he was just trying to butter you up?" April asked. "So he could get what he wanted?"

Depressing the corners of my mouth, I shrugged my shoulders and shook my head.

I think a woman is dead, I said...

CHAPTER FORTY-SEVEN

"You are really stretched thin," said my therapist. "You take care of this really needy population who's always asking things of you. You're reaching out to this native population to try to help them, even when they don't really want your help. You're taking on these book projects that are taking up all your time outside of work. Trying to help this medical assistant who got hurt. You're trying to keep friendships together. You're just dealing with all of this heavy stuff. So I think it's OK that you look forward to something that's light, and fun and entertaining and an escape."

I described my birthday party at the Capitol Garage, and the feelings for Mercury I awoke to the next morning.

"And what do you think about that?" she asked. "If you were going to give that feeling a name, what would you call it?"

Maybe 'Justice', I responded. 'Serves you right.'

"Why would it say that?"

Because of the way I let go of my first love, Bubbles.

"So it sounds like you feel like you're being punished for something in the past?"

I nodded.

Yes, I said.

"On the one hand, I don't believe that," she responded. "But on the other, I'm curious why you feel that way?... It sounds like you're being really hard on yourself. I would say, Appreciate yourself. For being who you are. What do you feel in your heart, Dave?"

Love, I answered. Love for everything. For everyone.

"Love for yourself?"

No, not for myself.

A feeling of hollowness surfaced in my chest. It was the same feeling as I'd had essentially my whole life, especially in high school.

"What strikes me with all the various things you're doing and what's going on, is that you're not appreciating yourself for what *you're* doing," she said. "Even with the opioids, you might not be totally fixing it, but you're doing something, instead of nothing. And you're not abandoning people – any of the various ones that you mentioned. Except yourself.

"It's just all sounds like you have really high expectations for yourself. Even thinking about your mother, you're doing what you can – What she will allow you to do."

"So be happy with what is, and what it may become," she concluded, "and really appreciate yourself..."

CHAPTER FORTY-EIGHT

I told April about the appointment with the therapist.

"Is that why you wear run down clothes?" she asked. "Because you don't love yourself? I always thought there was some kind of self-worth issue with you doing that."

I considered my admiration for Mercury. His exuberance and ability to look me in the eye. Then, I felt frustrated about my mangled body, with muscles that wouldn't do what I wanted the way Mercury's would.

"The funny thing is," April inserted, "I don't think that Mercury is free of trauma. Obviously not. He broke a rib. But he still going on. Maybe the trauma didn't affect him the same way that it affected you? Or he's more resilient? Younger?"

Yes, I thought. Perhaps I could learn from him about being more fearless and having fun with people?

"So why don't you say that to him?" she implored. "Say like, 'There's all these things that I really appreciate about you. One is your resilience. Another is your insistence on doing what you want to. And I'm just in awe of your amazing dancing. I wish I could do that, but I had an accident, and I just can't get out of it enough to have your perfect posture, and every time I watch you, I'm just in awe of the way you carry yourself and the way you move your body.' Just say it – Plain speaking."

"Then you would know you said it," she concluded. "You could ask, 'Do you have any tips?'..."

CHAPTER FORTY-NINE

Reports from my brother indicated that my mom was getting worse.

She thinks she is smart but she doesn't make a bit of sense
If only I could get as far away from here as u brother

Months before I'd gone to L.A. intent on convincing her about the importance of taking her pills. But she refused, and, per the dictates of my profession, I reported it, and it had been eating me since.

"Dave, you called protective services and all they did was knock on the door," April said. "And when your mom didn't answer it, they left. And it cost you big time, because now she really doesn't want to see you.

"But you had to do it, because if anyone were to come back legally and say, 'Why did you not talk to them?' You can say, 'I talked to protective services, and after I called protective services, my mom got very distrustful. She has trust issues. Documented trust issues. Clinical trust issues. And after I called protective services, she did not trust me anymore, and did not want me around.'"

Nodding, I still had doubts about what I'd done...

Leaving the house, I went skating. Standing to the side as the children played limbo, I squatted to relieve the tension in my back; but when I rose to stand up again, I became lightheaded and fell to the ground.

Looking up from the floor, I wondered how long I'd been out? And if anyone had seen me? And whether this qualified as true loss of consciousness and had to be reported?...

CHAPTER FIFTY

Preparing to leave for this week's drag show, April thought it would be fun if we came in wigs.

Sure, I responded. Maybe it would help me blend into the crowd, instead of looking like such an old man.

But despite a blond wig covering most of my face, within the first number Mercury was gliding a knowing finger to part the 'hair' from my eyes.

After the show April sent me onstage to get a photo with Mercury and the other drag queens. Standing with him, I told him that before the show April had wondered if he'd recognize me with the wig on?

"Oh, please," Mercury responded. "I've seen enough 'bobs' in my life that I can tell what's under a wig."

The other drag queen laughed.

"I think he's probably a 'bob'," she commented…

"What's a 'bob'?" April asked later. "You should have asked them."

Googling it, she reacted with hysterical laughter.

"'Bob is an acronym for a bend over buddy'," she read. "I'm sure that's not what they meant."

I'm not, I responded.

She continued researching.

"'Big old bitch'… 'Battery operated boyfriend'… Well, you might want to ask them."

And I might not…

CHAPTER FIFTY-ONE

In the morning I awoke to discover that our cat, Queenie, had peed all over the papers next to my desk.

April laughed.

"As well as struggling with a human queen, you're struggling with a cat queen," she said, "who is providing plenty of excitement for you, so that if you don't get out of bed within five minutes of her jumping on you, there was punishment coming."

Collecting the papers, I deposited them outside.

"When you get a dull animal, they just follow whatever you want them to," April continued. "But when you have a cat that's 'all there', and she is an independent creature, then you wind up with a cat like Queenie, and you have to work on her terms and conditions – Like working with a CEO."

"I don't think I ever told you this," she confided. "When we were visiting Rosebud on our site visit, they had us walking around the hospital housing near where Esther lived. And I remembered watching this tomcat. It was like an orange tabby cat. It was in the tall grass, so all I could see was its head. And he was looking in every which direction, and his ears were twitching. He was really 'there', and making his own decisions. And I didn't know if it was a stray or if it was a pet. And I looked at that cat, and I was like, 'That cat is really something. It's really making its own decisions. He is all there. I want a cat like that.'"

"And, lo and behold," she concluded, "a year later, I had a cat like that."

Be careful what you wish for, I thought...

CHAPTER FIFTY-TWO

Where everyone had been so nice last week about me showing up in a wig, April thought we'd take it a step further and put me in women's clothing as well this time.

"Take advantage of this gender bending adventure," she declared, "and come wearing a dress. After all, they're so open to people in drag they take off the cover charge for anyone in a drag outfit."

April suggested the costume I wore a couple years ago for the Halloween Party at IHS Headquarters. Back then, I oversaw LGBTQ Office, and when I floated the idea of cross-dressing for the party, the staff applauded.

"Dr. Fischer, if you dress up as a woman," the LGBTQ Director declared, "I will love you forever..."

But the gown was too ghoul-like, so April suggested I use one of her dresses. Searching her closet, we found a red-and-black party dress that went with my 'Enchantress' wig (brunette with red highlights).

Then, April had another idea.

"Gosh, Dave, I wonder what you would look in this wig?"

It was the bleach blonde one she'd worn for Halloween.

"Why don't you try it?" she asked.

I'd found it less than appealing on her (I thought it made her look like Cloris Leachman from *Phyllis)* and being that we had similar features, I was expecting it would elicit the same reaction when I put it on me.

But looking in the mirror, I experienced something entirely different: Instead of repelled, I was immediately put at ease. It felt like I was looking at a 'lighter', more relaxed version of myself.

And the effect was transforming – Like someone opened an escape valve to my system and released all the pressure.

April commented that the red and black dress didn't go with the blond wig.

"Let me put you in another dress and see how you look then," she said.

She selected a dark dress that was not unlike the traditional military dress portrayed in Korean historical dramas, like the one we'd seen last night, which featured April's favorite Korean actor (who she had a crush on and binge-watched all his movies). Then, applying the blond wig, I seemed to transform again – This time looking like a cross between a goth anime character and April's Korean actor!

Seeing me walk into the hallway, April put a hand to her heart, then doubled over, as though receiving a jolt though her solar plexus...

CHAPTER FIFTY-THREE

April took photos from different angles of me in the goth blond anime outfit. Looking at them I was shocked at the kink in my neck! I looked like Quasimodo, and wondered that April or any of my friends or family could let me walk around that way?

"I think I've said gentle things to you about that before," she responded. "To walk this way or that. But I think that when you wear your male clothes, it's not as apparent. They're more forgiving at that. Whereas female clothes are more slicker aligned, so that it's easier to see your posture."

The kink looked to be right at the place where that bully from school dug his thumb into my neck.

But whatever the source, I didn't want what I saw. Not for one minute.

I have to let it go, I thought. It was neither productive, nor who I am, nor want to be. Just a source of stress...

CHAPTER FIFTY-FOUR

"You're figuring out what this is about," Carl commented. "It's really something. It says to me that you're ready to lose the inhibitions, and you're not afraid to explore different things that you haven't explored yet. It's incredibly liberating."

"Congratulations," he continued. "You're breaking through something. It will be interesting to see where it goes. But even more, you're breaking free. Freer and freer. You're feeling calmer. Like that pressure inside is just being released. Like the tire just going down – *hiss!* - to absolute release.

"And April's on a journey here, too... By being supportive of you, instead of something bad happening, it seems that just the opposite occurred. Like, 'Wow, look at what I have, too.' And therefore, instead of the realization of your worst fears, it becomes the fulfillment of your dreams."

"Yeah, my fantasy husband," April responded. "It was amazing to look at Dave. Here my husband is looking at me in my house, and he is having the look of my fantasy historical actors. And it was like, 'Wow, I have it right here.'"

"It was pretty intense," she concluded. "I was pretty attracted..."

CHAPTER FIFTY-FIVE

Parking a few blocks from the Capitol Garage, I got out to pay the meter. But it wasn't reading my credit card, so I asked April for hers. It was already dark and a stocky fellow approached us and asked if we could use a light? But just then, the card took and I told him we were okay. A moment later (after we'd turned to make our way to the restaurant), April broke out in laughter.

"Didn't you hear what that guy said?" she asked. "I can't believe that you missed it! You totally weren't paying attention!... He said, 'Girls, do you need some help?' And you didn't turn around, but you answered him in a voice that was really deep and go, 'No, I'm okay.' And it startled him, and he steps back, then turns around and walks away. And he just had this look on his face like, 'I'm getting out of here.'"

She continued laughing.

"It was the best thing ever," she exclaimed. "It was such the best thing ever. Oh my God..."

Entering the diner, it took a moment for the host to recognize me, and he, too, seemed taken aback.

"So, you see, Dave," April announced after we were seated. "If you dress right, I'm sure you'd get guys going after you all over the place. You're a slim, blond-haired woman."

She smiled.

"I wonder what that guy's going to tell his friends?" she mused. "'I saw this pretty chick, then I went up to her, and she was a man!'"

She laughed.

"I wonder if now he thinks I'm a man, too..."

CHAPTER FIFTY-SIX

Mercury kicked off the show with an act that displayed his usual uncanny strength, agility and balance – contorting his body backwards till his back was near parallel with the floor, before pulling himself upright again.

But the highlight of the evening belonged with another performer – Tilly Creams – who danced to Lady Gaga's *Applause.* Though more compact than Mercury, he was just as supple, athletic, charismatic and steady on his feet. At the song's climax he performed a cartwheel right into a death drop, igniting cheers from the crowd...

After the show Tilly appeared while we were waiting for Mercury. Pulling Tilly aside I tipped him, saying I appreciated his performance. He responded full of gratitude, spontaneity and joy.

"If you want to see me again," he said, smiling, "I'm at Faces most Saturdays."

As with Mercury I was taken by his warmth and friendliness and felt drawn.

How far does this go? I wondered...

Mercury appeared not long after. He had taken off his makeup and appeared quite handsome – which surprised me because in photos without makeup posted on social media, I thought he looked rather plain and sensitive, with a sleepy-eyed look that was not at all the way he looked in costume – or now! – when he looked so alive. I was reminded of photographs I'd seen of my friend, Ethel: When she was younger, she had a similar sleepy look; as opposed to later photos when she looked vital and alive. Looking at those pictures I'd wondered when was the time that she'd 'awakened' and what was the source of the change? In Mercury's case, I thought there wasn't much question – It was drag!...

April pulled Mercury aside and related that she thought I needed to choose a drag name that would create a persona around the blond wig.

"But we're having a hard time picking one," she said.

"I say for the first name, go with your first street address," Mercury offered, "and for your last name, go with the name of your first pet."

The street where I grow up was Allott Avenue. My first pet was a dog named Blackie.

A-LottA Black? I thought, doubtful.

Mercury commented on my dress.

"I suggest you shop at Rainbow," he said. "There's one on Watt Avenue."

April laughed.

"At this point," she responded, "Dave is raiding my closet."

"Yeah, that's how I started," he responded. "I started by raiding my mom's closet. Now, I make my own. Like this one." He indicated the two-piece skirt he was wearing. "I sowed it this morning."

"Where did you get the fabric from?" April asked.

"Well, it was the only roll in Walmart that wasn't glued down, so I stole it," he responded. "Just kidding. My favorite place is Hi-Fashion..."

Mercury took his leave.

"He was quite relaxed with us," April commented. "More relaxed than he's ever been before. I wonder if that's because he was accepting you as a baby drag?..."

CHAPTER FIFTY-SEVEN

The following morning April smiled.

"It was so fun to kiss a girl yesterday," she said, laughing. "A girl with a deep voice and a five-o'clock shadow."

She asked if I wanted to go with her to the fabric store Mercury had told her about?

"I know he doesn't have a lot of money," she said. "We know he lost his job and wrecked his car a while back. I know you want to support him, and I was just remembering, as an artist, I really appreciated when people supported my art and the art I was making, and maybe we could get him a gift certificate? This way we could be a patron of his art and it's not so personal. It will be sort of a gift for us, because we'll get to see what he makes out of it..."

Purchasing the certificate, April then sought the perfect card, as well as decorative bag and wrapping paper.

"I like him, too," she insisted. "And I saw him first. I told you about him..."

Afterwards, April suggested we follow his advice and look for drag-wear at the Rainbow Shop. But I wasn't impressed with the selection, and we left empty-handed.

Then, April spotted a Ross across the way...

"So we go to Ross," April told Carl, "and there are racks and racks and racks of discounted female clothes. So there are zillions of them, and Dave was in seventh heaven. And I'm like, 'Why are you so happy?' And he said, 'Look at all these colors. Look at all these patterns. I'm so excited I can be here picking these things for me to wear.'"

Carl responded as though tongue-tied.

110

"Right," he said. "Yes. Yes."

"And that gave him a lot of satisfaction," April continued. "Like that was something he's not used to when he shops for himself. And it's something he wants."

"Because of what's available?" Carl asked.

Yes, I said. In the men's aisle everything struck me as utterly boxy, uninteresting, colorless clothes. So, yes, it was exhilarating (indeed, 'liberating') to experience what you can purchase and potentially wear if you're willing to pick something from the women's aisle.

"And the funny thing is," April inserted, "I like a lot of what he chooses. And actually my favorite dress right now is a dress he picked for himself – And I took over!"

"Oh, wow!" Carl responded, stunned. "Wow. So this is – This is you exploring! It feels very free. It feels very authentic. It feels good…"

CHAPTER FIFTY-EIGHT

Skiing with Sam again, I recounted the experience of looking at myself in the mirror wearing the blond wig and the feeling of ease that came over me?

"I was thinking how physical appearance can change things," he responded. "Or just looking at things differently. Especially in a surprised sense, when you weren't expecting it. It kind of opens your eyes – 'Wait a minute, I can be a totally different person just by manipulating my appearance.'

"Of course you don't change who you are internally. But then, maybe you do? And very few people have gone through this experience. Most people are scared to go through this."

"What did you see when you saw yourself?" he inquired. "Was it you? Or was it someone else?"

It was a relaxed version of myself, I said. Like someone who didn't live a 'heavy' life. Where there weren't the whys and wherefores in every interaction – Conditions and due diligence ('I'll give you Viagra, but you can't use Meth or cocaine') and I could just be.

"I think we put so much pressure on ourselves," he responded. "To be somebody, and then you realize, 'Wait a minute, I am more than what I think I am.' And those pressures that are associated with a certain image of yourself, you realize, 'Wait a minute, I'm more than just that image. I'm not just this one type of person. I am not constrained by being a certain type of person that people expect me to be.' You're not locked into it, just because your dad told you, 'You should be a doctor.' 'I can go in different directions. I don't have to walk this very rigid path, which is stressful. There is more to me. I can realize more of my potential.'

"It's neat that you can see yourself in so many different ways. It's like a diamond with the different facets. You can do that. You can push yourself to so many different boundaries, so that you can grow, and still be productive."

"I think that what you're doing is going through an adventure," he concluded. "And I think that's neat, because it shows you don't have to take a plane or travel far to have an adventure. You can do it right in your backyard – at a place where you're being entertained!..."

CHAPTER FIFTY-NINE

The week's drag show started with Mercury donning a red wig. Watching him I flashed to Nikki (who was red-haired) and recalled the events of the last time I saw her.

"I used to dance at a place like this," she'd said of the restaurant we'd stopped at on the way home from our ill-fated camping trip. "I fell off a stage not very different from this one and hurt my leg."

Gazing at the stage I imagined her falling and felt sad. She and my father had argued earlier in the day, and seated next to her at the table, I asked what would happen now?

"I don't know," she responded. "This might be our last supper…"

"So Nikki was your dad's ex-girlfriend?" Dino asked later. "He left your mom for this chick, right?"

Yes, I said. Her memory still haunts me, in part because I still blame myself for her death.

"Why?" he asked.

Because she didn't like kids, I responded. She saw no point in having them, and I thought my brother and me were the reason she and my father broke up.

"Why do people have children?" she asked me pointedly that last camping trip.

I'd shrugged my ten year old shoulders.

"Maybe because they want company," I responded.

She threw her head back.

"That's selfish!" she declared. "If you want company, get a dog!…"

"I don't know," Dino commented later. "People have kids by accident. People have kids because they want to pass on their genes. People have kids for all sorts of reasons. Not all of them are great, but that sucks that that sticks in your head."

I recalled a conversation with my mother about Nikki.

"She came and picked you up," my mother began. "I saw her for ten seconds or less. You were like five years old. When you came home, you told me she paraded around you naked. You think I like to hear that?... Little children don't need women – adults – that are so stupid that they parade around naked in front of children who don't even know them. Who are influenced and impressionable at that young age. I feel for children, and I feel for you. Because, believe me, she wasn't nice. Her face wasn't nice, either. It was like hard. She had a hard face. It may have been an attractive face, but it was hard.

"I told your dad and he said that would never happen again. But, later, he came around, and fooled around, asking me for money – saying he needed it because his girlfriend wanted a boob job, and was a topless dancer..."

"Was she a stripper?!" Dino exclaimed. He broke into laughter. "That's pretty interesting right there. You like admired her as a dancer, and your mom is like, 'No, she was a stripper.' It's like, Oh, there's a little different connotation..."

My thoughts drifted to Mercury: The first time I saw him, I thought he was a dancer and had no clue he was a drag queen – though, according to April, it was obvious.

"He was not wearing open-chested overalls," she'd said disparagingly. "It was a dress..."

Dancer becomes stripper? Dancer becomes drag queen?

But as much as I strained to consider the parallels, my mind drew a blank...

CHAPTER SIXTY

Heavy rains were probably responsible for the sparse crowd at the Capitol Garage. Still, it was a quality show, with Apple Adams performing side-by-side with Mercury...

"If you want to see us together again," Mercury commented after the show, "we'll be at Badlands on Monday."

"We'd like to," April responded, "but Dave works."

Concerned that Mercury still hadn't acquired gainful daytime employment, I sent April a darting glance.

But Mercury took no offense.

"Yeah, I really shouldn't stay out that late either," he responded...

"Did all that touching make you feel again?" April asked after Mercury departed. "Because he was really laying it on thick! He was rubbing all up and down your arm. Doing this."

She demonstrated, laughing.

"Like with me, he's sweet," she continued. "But with you, he's sultry..."

CHAPTER SIXTY-ONE

April confided that she'd bumped Mercury's chin while exchanging hugs.

"I sent him an invitation to friend me on Facebook," she added. "I wanted to tell him I was sorry for bumping him on the chin when I was talking to him. I sent it along with a picture of you, so he would know who we were... It's the photo we took on our drive up north to Indian territory. I've already got some comments. Kelly 'liked' that photo... Kelly from the Red Roof Inn."

Kelly was the hotel manager there. She'd been very good to us the year we'd lived in that hotel while I was working at IHS headquarters in DC before we came here.

"She had a crush on you," April said. "She was jealous of me..."

By morning Mercury had responded to April's apology with a message on Facebook.

LOL. No worries. I'm a durable queen.

"But he didn't 'friend' me," April commented, disappointed. "And I don't know why, because he has over fifteen hundred friends."

"Even though he didn't friend me," she added, "I still know where he lives... Because I'm smart – and a little creepy."

"On a video he was outside talking about the homeless situation where he lives," she explained. "I thought, 'I wonder if I can find his apartment complex?' And I did.

"I knew the main street, and then I saw that there was a bridge crossing it. And whenever I found bridges, I'd look for apartment complexes there. I knew the façade of the buildings of his apartment, so I looked for what the houses look like at those apartment complexes on their websites and I matched it. So I know exactly where he lives. He gave enough information in his videos for someone to find him."

She laughed.

"Probably nobody is that stalky of him," she continued. "But I couldn't help myself. I was looking at that video, and saying to myself, 'I bet I can find where he lives.' Because you and I have been worried about where he lives. And I wanted to find out the crime rate there.

"So when I pinpointed where he lived, I found out the crime rate. And it is very crimey he where he lives. It's one of the worst areas."

Then, she hesitated.

"Do you think I crossed a line there?" she asked. "It's not like I'm going to go and knock on his door or anything."

No, it obviously came from a place of caring...

CHAPTER SIXTY-TWO

"We're going to take a short intermission," Mercury announced, "and if any of you need to use the facilities, we just have one gender neutral bathroom, so no smoking, no fornicating or indulging in other sex acts in there, or else the drag queens will join you and it will get really weird..."

The reason for the single restroom was because the drag queens had sequestered the men's room for dressing changes. So when I told April I was going to use it, she insisted on coming with me.

Entering the restroom, we found all three stalls occupied. Then, before we could exit, three young women walked inside. Seeing them, I panicked and made to rush out.

But the young women just smiled and spoke reassuringly.

"It's OK," said one.

"We can wait," said another.

"It's no problem," said the third.

Entering a vacated stall, I couldn't bring myself to go standing up. But when I sat, I was surprised to find the bowl wet!...

"Most women squat when they pee," April explained. "To keep from getting germs and contracting disease."

I lifted my brows and shrugged.

Well, I guess I'm contracting disease, I responded...

CHAPTER SIXTY-THREE

Returning to my chair I considered how at ease those young woman were with me in the restroom.

How could they be so utterly unfazed?! I thought.

Just then, the lights faded and Mercury came out onstage in a miniskirt, dancing to Shania Twain's *Man! I Feel Like A Woman.*

The best part of being a woman
Is the prerogative to have a little fun, and...

As the chorus played Mercury leapt from the stage and kissed the cheek of each person at the bar.

Oh, oh, oh, really go wild.
Yeah, doin' it in style...

The crowd howled for more, particularly the young women.

Then, stepping back onstage, Mercury stripped off the miniskirt to reveal a pair of cut-off shorts underneath – and though more tame than what I was expecting (I thought he'd have only a G-string), the thrusting of his hips left my jaw dropped, thinking, 'This is no woman!'

"Mercury is not repressed!" April declared. "He might be sensitive like you are, but he is not submissive..."

Just then, I heard a 'thump' – like a bowling ball striking the ground – and instantly (from my years of having worked in nursing homes) I knew what that meant – Namely, someone had just collapsed, hitting his or her head against the floor!

Leaping from my chair I dashed in the direction of the sound, till locating a man on the ground still convulsing from an apparent seizure...

Later, as I stood overseeing the man's safe loading unto an awaiting ambulance, I became aware of aches in my sides, and imagined they came from numerous unintended elbows I'd taken on the way to the fallen man.

I might be repressed, I thought, but I'm not so inhibited that I'll let it get in the way of assisting someone in need.

Just then, Mercury's tall, slender frame came into view, effortlessly gliding towards me.

"Thanks for saving the day," he said, softly. "When I saw that fella go down, I thought, 'That doesn't look good.'

"But, then, I looked again and saw you there, and thought, 'Oh, we're okay.'..."

CHAPTER SIXTY-FOUR

Standing naked in a church with the sound of Celine Dion's *My Heart Will Go On* playing in the background, I saw Sandra and Tommie (the middle daughter and older son of my old girlfriend, Kate) standing by a pew. They were both children again, and Tommie was reaching for something (maybe gum) in his pocket. I was concerned he might get in trouble; but he just turned and maturely led his sister to the end of the pew and the two sat; then, when he got up again, he transformed from a little boy to an adult.

A commotion followed and it seemed the congregants had risen with a stir and were advancing on either me or Mercury? A moment later, though, they were flailing on the ground, seizing, and it was announced overhead that God had it in for them...

Awakening from the dream, I pondered its meaning? There was the seizing man from the night before, and then (when Mercury removed his wig to conclude the show and then turned to leave the stage) I'd noted the shaved design of a small cross on the back of his head. At the time I'd wondered what message he was sending and whether it had something to do with a recent call by Pope Francis for tolerance towards the LGBTQ community?

"Who am I to judge?" the Pope said...

Tommie and I were in occasional contact, but he hadn't responded to my invitations to ski.

Sandra, meanwhile, had called me the other day to ask for medical advice about her infant son, Franklin, who'd been running a fever. Talking with her, I'd wondered how she and her brothers and sisters would react to my feelings for Mercury, especially given their Catholic upbringing?

Then, as though right on cue, Kate's youngest daughter, Alyssa, texted.

How are things with you? I am home in Tennessee visiting for a week. I got here about a day ago. It's been ok. I love being with Franklin. Sometimes I'm not sure why I feel like I just can't be satisfied. Like things that would make a normal person just super happy about, im kind of just like eh

I responded by telling her that people's reactions were different, and how recently after a lifetime of following the standard advice to take a deep breath when anxious, I'd discovered that taking the opposite tack and letting go of a breath and exhaling was more relieving.

I will try it! Thanks for the advice. I'll take any tips I can get.

There's nothing to try, I responded. I just meant to say that sometimes you can have expectations about how you're going to feel when you do something, and if it turns out you don't feel as you expected, maybe you could just take that in, reflect on it, and perhaps try something else, and see how that makes you feel?...

"Who are you texting?" April asked.

Alyssa, I answered. I was about to tell her about Mercury.

"Your ex-girlfriend's very Catholic daughter?!" April exclaimed. "Who was considering becoming a nun?... Dave, for years you were like a father to those kids. You still have a relationship with them that's important to you – That you value. Telling them something like that could jeopardize it. Do you really think that's a good idea?"

My heart sank in my chest. I'd be crushed if the kids stopped conversing with me; when April and I were in South Dakota, I'd send them photos of the same bridge at sunset nearly every day, and their constant good cheer and interest helped me through those difficult years.

Still, more than a 'father figure', I'd always strived to be open and honest with them – And not hold back, but, rather, speak from the heart.

"Of late, I've had a wild experience," I wrote. "I was at the art museum for an event, and by chance saw a drag queen dance, and was so impressed by his ability that I wanted to see him perform again. And between his talent and getting to know him, I've fallen in love. Since then, I've had lots of questions about what I'm feeling – And nothing about my life has really changed, except perhaps a greater ability to love."

Awaiting a response, I wondered that April was right, and I should have been more 'protective', and not challenged Alyssa so much?

Then, a reddish pink heart appeared next to my text.
Wow that is a wild and great experience! Thanks for sharing...

CHAPTER SIXTY-FIVE

At a gay nightclub called The Depot, Mercury was hosting a watch-party for the hit TV program *RuPaul's Drag Race.* Sitting atop a platform with another drag queen (Aurora Lot MooRe), Mercury was all smiles – waving to us as we entered the establishment – though made-up like some haunted figure.

"I bet you like that," April commented.

When I indicated I didn't (Saying I wasn't into scary stuff), she looked at me perplexed.

"What happened to the guy who showed up at the Purim party twenty years ago as a skeleton?" she asked. "Our first picture that we have together – the one and only picture we took together way back when we were in DC – you face-painted yourself like a skull."

I'd wanted to make a blowup of that photo for our wedding, but April objected, saying her family (many of whom were the descendants of Holocaust victims) avoided all things implying death.

"My sister and I were kind of horrified," she continued. "Because you didn't know about Purim I guess, and thought it was Halloween."

Yes, I treated it like a costume party, I conceded.

"But it was Purim," she responded. "You don't do that on Purim. Girls get dressed up as queens and princesses and butterflies. And boys get dressed up as clowns. Purim isn't about the undead and skeletons and witches. You do that on Halloween."

She hesitated.

"But I have to admit," she softened, "that I did go as a witch. Because I didn't have a costume, and my roommate had a costume, so I think I remade it, and took her gown, and then made the witch's hat with stars on it. So I think it became more like an astronomer."

I thought she looked like a fairy princess.

"You thought I was a fairy princess?!" she exclaimed, her *features noticeably brightening...*

After the *RuPaul* episode the chairs and tables in the club were rearranged so that Mercury and Aurora could perform a short drag show.

Mercury danced first. Taking the bills I held out to him, he kneeled and kissed my hand. Smiling, I wanted to kneel, too, and tell him, 'Queens don't kneel to their humble subjects...'

Aurora was next. Bold and exotic, she struck me as nothing less than a force of nature, as she danced about the room like a whirling dervish.

Then, in what seemed a natural consequence of the spontaneous combustion she ignited in the crowd, Aurora stripped off her dress.

As I looked on fretting over what would happen next, Mercury just clapped his hands and gleefully joined in – Removing his outfit, too, and putting on Aurora's.

But Aurora's performance wasn't finished yet, and the next part involved applying mayonnaise to her hair, then taking the first available article of clothing at her disposal and wrapping it around her head like a turban.

The problem was, it was Mercury's top she'd sequestered, leaving Mercury with nothing to wear, and having to go the rest of the evening bare-chested in only his high heels and miniskirt.

"Do you think that was total payback?" April asked. "Because Mercury had been upstaging Aurora most of the night?"

But Mercury appeared not the least bit perturbed, and went about laughing and smiling and freely conversing with the crowd...

CHAPTER SIXTY-SIX

Traveling to an Opioid Crisis Roundtable in the Bay Area, I spent most of the two-hour drive talking with my colleague, Matt. Matt was familiar with my ongoing efforts to advance alternative modalities for the treatment of pain, and I'd demonstrated energy work to him. After sharing about physical activities I was doing (from skiing to skating to dance) to challenge myself, I got around to the subject of Mercury.

"I want to learn from him," I said. "But his abilities so exceed my own that I feel like why even try?"

Matt smiled.

"What you're saying kind of reminds me of a story about Vincent van Gogh," he said. "His doctor did painting on the side and always wanted to be an artist. Then, he saw Vincent's work, and he was like, 'I'm never going to paint again', because it was that extraordinary."

I nodded. By coincidence, the other night Mercury had performed in a mini-dress featuring a rendering Van Gogh's *Starry Night*.

"Do you like the outfit?" he'd asked. "It makes me feel artistic…"

Matt's comment also led me to remember a conversation I'd had with an art store owner about healers.

"She said she was attending classes by a 'guru'," I recalled, "and he was performing these extraordinary acts of healing. But, at the same time, she said he had these significant personal foibles that she couldn't understand. 'How could someone so gifted and enlightened be so flawed?' she thought. But, later, she said it was helpful – because she realized where he might be better at some things, she was still better at others, and that gave her what she needed – like 'permission' – to strike out and help people on her own."

"Do you know what this 'guru' was teaching?" Matt asked.

She hadn't said, but I imagined it was something like the energy work I do.

"When I teach bioenergy," I asserted, "I tell people that they might be the one person in the world who can really make a difference in another person's life. I'd felt that way when I was caring for my friend, Ethel. There was essentially no one else caring for her – this despite a church full of friends and admirers who came to her funeral. Before that, I'd never met any of them."

"When you say 'spend time'," Matt inquired, thoughtfully, "was that your spending time talking? Or doing energy work?"

Both, I responded, though I thought our conversations were especially helpful in reconciling the events of her life.

"Do you think our interpersonal relationships make an impact on the energy body?" he asked.

My mind drifted to the exchange with Alyssa from the other day.

"Every time I'm home and I go to Sonic," she'd texted, *"I think of you and how you'd take us every time after tennis. We really appreciated all you did for us as kids. You made our childhood so much fun where otherwise I don't think it would've been."*

I described the recent dream with Sandra and Tommie, and said I thought it spoke to my lingering regrets about leaving Tennessee?

Well if you hadn't left Tennessee you wouldn't have went to all the other places and experienced those things and met people! But we did have a good time when you lived in Tennessee.

Yes, though I was finding myself wishing now that I could live my life more like a spirit – everywhere and with everyone at once.

If only!...

"Yes," I told Matt. "I believe our relationships have the greatest impact on the energy body as a whole. Indeed, it seems to me that the energy impression I leave behind is the most important thing I'll do…"

Jewish Film Festival & Dance

Please join us at the West Theatre, Saturday evening, March 9th.
There will be dancing at the reception from 6-7PM.
Music will be performed by the Klezmer band.
Saturday ticket pass includes reception, Havdalah service and three movies.
Hope to see you there for all the fun...

CHAPTER SIXTY-SEVEN

I'd been slated to perform with the local Israeli Dance troupe for the opening of the Jewish Film Festival at the Crest Theatre. I hadn't danced with the troupe for a while and worried I'd be rusty.

"Just let out your 'inner Mercury'," April told me.

April videoed the event while I dance with the others. Flowing with the music as the klezmer band played, I embraced the joy of dancing amongst friends...

"I was watching you dance from the balcony," a woman told me after. "I think we all were. You must be the most graceful person I've ever seen. Your energy is so uplifting. Is there somewhere that you dance?"

Smiling, I gave her the time and location of the weekly dance class.

"And you go there?" she asked, insistent...

A blond woman edged closer till standing eye-to-eye with me and well within my personal space.

"Thank you," she said, slipping a folded paper into my hand.

The best part – ? Watching you dance. Love C! 602-...

Whoa! I thought, raising my eyelids.

Showing it to April, she laughed.

"I like to watch your butt," April commented. "As I sat there videoing you and the others dancing, I was actually concentrating on how you were moving your butt. If you were still sexually attracted to me, that would definitely be a way to get me in bed. The way you move your butt in a good way. You do it good."

"And your hands are graceful – like a dancer. Graceful and beautiful. I love that. Oh, but the butt is sexy. If we're talking sex..."

She laughed again.

It was nice to hear, given how intimidated I'd become of Mercury. I couldn't imagine he'd think much of my dancing.

"Ohhhh," she said, sympathetically. "I don't know. He's never really seen you glide. He's never seen you do Israeli folk dancing – or skating. That's when you really engage that grace. That more lyrical part of you.

"You have a lyrical kind of way of moving when you do Israeli folk dancing and when you skate that might not be totally apparent when you do just free dancing, or when you're trying to do what he does. I mean, what he does is completely different from what you do. And when you were trying to do what he does… Well, practice makes perfect. And you also don't have quite the right mindset for it. So you're a novice and you're not quite, quite into it. But with other forms of dance, you're lyrical!"

"His kind of dance is a man trying to dance like a woman," she continued. "It means understanding the way a man and a woman dance, and intentionally moving like a woman. That's what all of the drag queens do. That's what all of them are working on - Is like being a man but moving like a woman.

"Your style of dancing combines both. And in some ways I think that's your problem so far with the drag stuff… You're both male and female as you dance. And they're striving for just female."

Yes, I certainly wasn't striving for that.

"Yeah. And I think you could. I think you probably could move just like a woman – if you put your mind to it. But that's not what your attitude is about. The way you dance it's not necessarily female and it's not necessarily male. It's more lyrical. Graceful. Like someone who doesn't have a sexual energy. I guess you're more androgynous. Yeah? Maybe? I don't know. Basically, you're a mix – *You Do Both.*"

I regarded her quizzically: It seemed only a short while ago that she'd said the same about Mercury?

"Yeah, but he's more female," she responded. "He doesn't physically change his body into female like the other drag queens do – except for tucking in and hiding his penis. He doesn't put on breasts or hips. He doesn't hide his muscular shoulders. He doesn't attempt to look like a voluptuous woman. But he moves like one. And he dresses like one. And he's excellent at that…"

CHAPTER SIXTY-EIGHT

Arriving at the Capitol Garage, the diner was already crowded.
April had called to say she was running late and might not make it, so
I told the host I'd wait at the bar rather than occupy a table.

Locating a space near the window, I ordered a drink, then buried
my head in a book. Not long after, though, a thin, sandy haired
young woman in a revealing, tight-fitting black jumpsuit came within
a foot of me, and, smiling, put a hand gently but firmly on my
shoulder.

"Hi," she said, assertively. "Can I bug you? I just did bath salts
and now I'm feeling like I could do everyone at this place. But look at
all these people – They're probably all gay. Are you gay?"

It happened that Mercury was standing directly in my line of
vision near the stage, and, seeing him, I responded to the woman by
saying I'd recently become aware that I was somewhere 'on the
spectrum', though I was also married.

"So you're a poly," she responded, matter-of-factly.

Resorting to the only 'Polly' I could think of, the image of a
cracker-seeking parrot perched on the shoulder of a pirate flashed in
my head.

"Polyamorous," she explained. "That you like being in more
than one relationship at the same time. Probably half the people in
this restaurant are that way."

Ahh, I said, nodding. That did sound like a pleasant way of
putting it.

Gesturing to the barstool tucked under the bar between us, I
asked if she'd like to have a seat?

"I can't sit down," she replied. "Not with this in my system."

I pulled back not a little startled – I'd heard about the aphrodisiac quality of bath salts, but beyond that my knowledge was rather vague.

"I'm not vague," she responded, still smiling, her hand on my shoulder. "You're vague."

Well, if not vague, then certainly square, I countered, wondering if she'd understand the reference and feeling ever more my age.

"Just tell me that you think I'm an asshole," she insisted, unperturbed. "I know I'm an asshole."

I thought nothing of the kind. Indeed, I liked her. Her hand still on my shoulder, I found her touch pleasant. She seemed a person who was living her life – at once cute and courageous, assertive yet disarming (though I did worry for her risk for contracting a sexually transmitted disease, however).

"You're a doctor, aren't you?" she asserted. "Probably Jewish, working for a humanitarian cause... Are Jewish people always into liberal stuff?"

I responded by recounting a story a homeless patient recently told me: He said he'd found a lawyer to do some *pro bono* work for him; when he learned the lawyer was Jewish, he asked why Jewish people always seem to go out of their way to help the underdog? In turn, the lawyer gazed over his shoulder, then looked back at my patient and said, "Because we always think we're next."

The young woman laughed.

"That's a good one," she said, smiling and looking more at ease.

Just then, the host inserted himself between us, saying this part of the bar was actually reserved and he'd have to seat me elsewhere...

Arriving later April laughed hysterically when I related the encounter.

"That's exactly the kind of thing a girlfriend might tell me," she said, catching her breath. "Like, 'This guy sat right next to me, and he was making a pass at me, and he wouldn't take no for an answer, and the waiter saved me.'"

It wasn't the waiter, I protested. It was the host.

"Do you think he noticed what was going on?" she asked. "And thought, 'Hey, I got to get him out of there'?"

I didn't know, though I did feel somewhat relieved being that this woman had come for a good-time and I was an utter stick in the mud.

April giggled.

"Is it OK that I said what I did?" she asked. "Or are you totally mad at me?"

It's fine, I said. By now I was fully aware that I was a girl.

"No, it's not that you're 'a girl'," she replied in nonjudgmental disgust. "It's just that our society is totally fucked up... It's expecting guys to have sex with anybody, and a girl to be more discerning. So, for a guy, if a girl starts something up like that, it's like, 'OK, scoring.' For a girl, it's like, 'Oh, he is like preying on me. I need to save myself.'"

"Basically, guys are supposed to be sluts," she concluded. "It's really weird..."

CHAPTER SIXTY-NINE

Taking the bills from my hand, Mercury clutched his heart, before then bending low and bestowing a kiss on April.

"It's cute how he kind of treats us equally," April said. "That when he does something with you, he does something with me."

Also performing was an older drag queen, who behaved like an airhead and even went by the stage name, Lucy Ludicrus.

"She'll stop Mercury at times," April commented, "and even Mercury will be like, 'What are you saying?'"

Nevertheless, Mercury treated Ludicrus with respect, saying she had helped him early in his career.

"This queen and I go way back," he announced. "OK, there was a time, when it was a little rough for me, and it was hard to pay the bills, and this entertainer – she stepped up, she helped out, and she pulled me through. So she's a close friend of mine…"

It was also the premier performance for a new drag queen from Folsom. Still a junior in high school, when he performed a death drop, he launched himself some five feet in the air before striking the ground – a feat that generated cheers from the crowd.

At the end of his performance Mercury hugged the young queen.

"So, is there any drag in Folsom?" Mercury asked him.

The young queen reacted by resignedly hanging his head, as though to signal something about the character of this town that was probably best known for its prison.

"Well, there's now drag in Folsom!" Mercury called out, triumphant, the crowd responding with liberal applause…

CHAPTER SEVENTY

"How are you, children?" Mercury asked, confidently striding towards us after the show.

I was reminded of Jasmine and her 'motherly' comments, and whether it was just a millennial tendency to conduct themselves more mature than those twice their age?

I remarked that young drag queen from Folsom was quite athletic.

"Yeah, I used to do a lot of risky stuff like that myself back in the day," Mercury responded. "I did all kinds of crazy shit when I was younger... I'm twenty-six now."

A veritable old man of the theatre, I thought, at less than half my age.

Accepting our usual contribution, Mercury held out two fingers.

"You're the best," he said.

Not knowing what to do, I met his fingers with my own, imagining it was some hip, young person's thing, to which I'd responded completely wrong...

CHAPTER SEVENTY-ONE

Together with Mercury, he was giving me the secret code for understanding cues and signs at a drag show.

Then, driving with Jasmine, she laughed in response to something I said. I was happy to see her smile, but became cognizant of an uncomfortable feeling in my chest and fearful that I might be on the verge of a heart attack?

Now at the Capitol Garage, Mercury was performing onstage, and my chest pain was getting worse. Recalling the fainting spell at The Rink, I crawled on all fours to the exit. I wanted to avoid causing a commotion and interrupting the show, but collapsed before I could pull myself through the doorway.

"Mercury, I'm so sorry," I said, terrified...

Awakening from the dream I experienced an odd sensation – like some opening in my chest.

Sitting up in bed I recalled a poem a former girlfriend composed for me.

When I am pressed close to your heart
And I hear its shallow beat
I think
'This man cannot love with this heart.
It is too weak.'

In the other room April lay sleeping with Sweetness. I confided that I was trying to detach from Mercury, but over and over he wins me with his ability and sweetness.

"He's just so cute!" April responded. "You got to admit you like him. I do, too..."

CHAPTER SEVENTY-TWO

On a walk to the park, our neighbor, Jeb, waved from his bike and pulled next to me on the sidewalk.

"Hi Dave," he said. "Haven't seen you in a while. What have you been up to?"

I responded that Sweetness was awaiting surgery. In the meanwhile April and I had taken up going to drag shows.

"I've been to a couple of drag shows before," he responded. "I enjoy them."

Then, he laughed.

"You should have seen my mother, Dave," he continued. "We went to a Sacramento gay men's chorale, and my mom had a ball. And the emcee there was a big busty woman in drag – well, actually he was a guy in drag. But he was a big busty woman, and she took to coming around to the audience and rubbing her breasts on the back of my neck. And there is my quaint, saintly, Baptist mother, laughing. I've never seen my mom laugh so hard."

Jeb's mother lived during the Depression. In photos from that time, she looked like a straight-laced woman right out of the pages of John Steinbeck's *Grapes of Wrath* (She'd actually come to California from Oklahoma to escape the Dust Bowl).

"She got to giggling," he continued. "She couldn't stop laughing. She just thought it was hilarious. We had a ball. It was a lot of fun."

I told him he and his wife should come see Mercury with us.

"I think I'll pass," he responded. "But let me know when you perform."

I said if that's what it took to get him to come, then, fine, I'll do it.

"Count us in then!" he exclaimed without a moment's hesitation. "Reckless abandonment and freedom of expression. Taking on a role so apart from your daily responsibilities. We'll be looking forward to it…"

CHAPTER SEVENTY-THREE

Relating the conversation with Jeb, April burst out in hysterical laughter.

"He is so awesome!" she said. "He is such an awesome friend. He's like, 'This is not for me, but if you make a fool of yourself, I want to be there. I'll support you.'"

She immediately went to the closet.

"Which dress do you want to wear?" she asked.

The red one, I responded.

"Well, that means I need to do laundry. And I need to give you some hose. And I have to get makeup…"

April left. Arriving home a few hours later, her face was covered in intense makeup.

"I went and got a little tutorial from a makeup artist who works in drag," she said. "And I got some makeup to put on you."

Though she spoke as though quite pleased, I was less than taken and thought the makeup left her appearing harsh.

April applied the makeup and lipstick to my face. The blond wig on my head, she said I looked handsome. But looking into the mirror, I experienced an intense feeling of deflation, as though all energy drained from my body.

"Do you want me to take the makeup off, Dave?" she asked.

No, I responded. I want to sit with this a while, so to figure it out.

Looking in the mirror again, it seemed that staring back at me was a sad clown – like the ones my grandfather used to paint (and I never liked) and hung all over the house – perhaps bringing back feelings of isolation and sadness that marked my youth.

"I think you look like your uncle," April commented.

Yes, my handsome uncle, whose sad, dejected expression pulled so many girls. I'd always envied him that – But now that I had that 'look', I couldn't wait to be rid of it.

If this is how my uncle feels, I thought, there's nothing to envy.

"Take the makeup off!" April cried. "This is supposed to be fun. If it's not fun, take it off."

But there was no time now. I'd waited too long and we needed to get going.

But heading to the car, I experienced an intense burning in my eyes and asked April to help me remove the makeup...

CHAPTER SEVENTY-FOUR

Arriving at the Capitol Garage Jeb and Julie were already seated at the table we'd reserved near the stage. Since they were sitting in the interior chairs within the cluster of other tables, there was no choice but for April and me to take the 'hot seats' along the aisle where the drag queens performed.

Introducing the show Mercury stammered through his usual opening comments.

"He keeps blowing his lines," April whispered. "I think he's high."

As the music started for his first number, Mercury appeared in a cheerleader's uniform to perform Katy Perry's *I Kissed a Girl*. I didn't think it was the most becoming outfit (Mostly, he looked like a male cheerleader). Also, I noted his eyes looked harder than usual – serious, businesslike, distant, perhaps because he was 'stoned' as April suspected. I did want to be supportive, though, and held out a couple bills.

C'mon, Mercury! I thought, smiling and nodding my head. Show'em what you can do!

He stopped then, and into my line of vision came a pair of parted purple lips till the image blurred in front of me! It was like something right out of the opening sequence of *The Rocky Horror Picture Show* – floating, painted lips filling the entire screen.

My thoughts went racing: 'This can't be happening. What am I going to do? Should I turn away? No, that's too prude. I'm going to do it.' At which point I closed my eyes and tilted my head.

A roar went through the crowd at the exact moment of contact. It was the same excited cry as when Mercury performed a death drop. But I was entirely unfazed, experiencing no startled excitement.

As he moved off, however, it struck me that I had friends sitting across the table, my wife seated next to me, and everyone at the restaurant, a witness. There could be no question as to my feelings now; perhaps before an entreaty for a kiss could be chucked up to jest; but this time it was different – Definite and unmistakable...

CHAPTER SEVENTY-FIVE

The rest of the evening I felt dazed and incapable of focusing on anything for any amount of time without my thoughts drifting to the kiss I shared with Mercury. Mercury, meanwhile, didn't seem to be fairing much better: Even after announcing the end of the show, the DJ came to him indicating there was a young women who'd just turned twenty-one, and her friends were requesting a lap dance to ceremonialize the occasion. Mercury looked weary as he acquiesced to the solicited exhibition. Nevertheless (as he'd demonstrated weeks earlier with April) his strength was such that all the time he was gyrating in this young woman's 'lap', he never made physical contact with her; instead, drawing from his seemingly boundless energy reserves to thrust his hips and shoulders from a low squat in a display of twerking that would have left the likes of Cardi B in stunned admiration.

"Well, that was awful," Mercury's only comment as he finished...

Jeb and Julie rose to take their leave; I asked them to stay for karaoke.

"I feel like I'm too old for this crowd," Jeb responded.

You're never too old, I pleaded, reassuringly. Age is but a state of mind.

But in spite my entreaties, they insisted on going and left with most of the other drag-goers.

Still, it was Saint Patrick's Day, and in place of those departing came nothing less than a tsunami of happy-go-lucky revelers (most of them already plied with drink) making their way through the door, seeking a new establishment to make merry in.

"Here to get fucked up?!" the DJ called out in greeting.

The bartenders appeared overwhelmed, doing everything they could to keep up with the seemingly unending calls for shots, ravenously consumed.

Still, even through the flood of spirits, an appreciation for art was not lost on the crowd: Returning to my seat after a rendering of Céline Dion's *My Heart Will Go On,* a tipsy young woman stumbled towards me.

"I liked that," she said, as though curiously amused at her own reaction. "I liked your singing…"

The next time the DJ called me up, a group of young people hopped onstage with me, and danced as I sang.

April was smiling, and despite my earlier misgivings about the makeup, she looked really attractive and having a thoroughly good time.

Mercury, though, still appeared out of it: Passing our table I held out our usual contribution; but unlike all the other times when he'd stop and talk, he just lifted the bills from my hand and kept moving.

I decided I was having too much fun to be bothered by it, nor would I give any more thought to events earlier in the evening.

April, however, knew otherwise.

"You'll probably be up thinking about him tonight," she said.

As usual, she was right…

CHAPTER SEVENTY-SIX

In the morning April asked about the kiss with Mercury? I said his lips were soft.

"Really?" she responded. "Somehow I wouldn't have expected that."

He'd made that way, I replied. Curling his upper lip.

"How long did it last?" she asked. "Was it really short?"

Long enough for those at all the tables around us to respond with a 'whoo' when we made contact.

"I didn't really hear that. I think I was like, 'Whoo.' Maybe I was one of the people 'whoo'-ing? Did they go 'whoo' when he kissed other people?"

I didn't recall, as I'd been rather stunned and left off-balance.

"He knows you want it," she said. "I think you're sending off energy saying, 'I'm interested in you sexually.'"

I thought I'd been sending energy saying I appreciate his dancing; however, it was a matter of public record that I had asked for a kiss (even if it was in jest).

"So maybe he's reacting to what you're sending?"

Very considerate of him, I said...

CHAPTER SEVENTY-SEVEN

Carl was anxious to get a report.

"How was the drag show?" he asked. "I want to hear all about it."

"Oh, I enjoyed it a lot!" April responded. "I went and got a little tutorial from a makeup artist who works in drag. And I got made-up, and I was having lots of fun.

"Because I grew up in a place where you didn't put on makeup. And if you did, it was very subtle and very sweet. So I actually don't even know how to put on makeup. That's why I went to have a makeup artist help me out. I didn't know anything about foundation. I didn't know where you put the rouge.

"I wasn't going to make myself pretty; I was going for theatrical. So I went overboard, with bold lipstick, fake eyelashes for the first time in my entire life, sparkle.

"And I told Dave that for me it's important to continue to explore putting theatrical makeup on because for me it's this getting over all these rules that I was raised with... 'A proper, modest girl does not do this type of stuff', and I don't want to be there anymore.

"And it has nothing to do with not being proper and sweet; I'm just refusing to take on these roles.

"Yes, yes," Carl said. "And you're experimenting with other parts of yourself."

"So I'm hoping that Dave can tolerate me putting on makeup," she continued.

I admitted that my initial reaction was that the makeup made April look severe - and that scared me.

"What do you mean severe?" Carl asked.

Someone who is harsh, angry, dark. Like perhaps the way I remember Nikki or even my mother in makeup.

And the odd thing was, though, that later on in the night I was taking pictures of April, and she looked really attractive, and fun in these photographs, and having a good time.

"I mean the fake lashes irritated my eyes," she said, "and taking off the makeup was awful. But I'm going to do it again, because it was fun…"

CHAPTER SEVENTY-EIGHT

"But now!" April continued, spiritedly. "The story continues! Mercury comes out for his first number lip-syncing, 'I Kissed a Girl and I liked it.' So he went over to Dave, who is all dressed in drag, and he goes in to kiss him, and they actually kissed on the lips – with Dave sitting next to me, and our friends across the table. And Dave told me later that after Mercury came in for the kiss, Dave was the one who moved his head forward to make contact."

She laughed.

"I was watching as Mercury moved on, and he actually moved in to kiss several people. I was too far away to see if he actually made lip contact with these other people. It was another drag queen that was there, and then a person who it seemed like Mercury knew. I think it was a total of four or five people that he went in for a kiss. But the kiss really took Dave on another emotional wind tunnel later on in the night.

"And the other interesting thing that happened was that Mercury was not chatty with us. I mean, he was a little chatty with me, but he would not talk with Dave afterwards. Like we went and did the photo, because obviously we were made-up. And Mercury kept complimenting my wig, because I had worn a rainbow wig, and he also hugged me. But he like kind of ignored Dave. All he said to Dave was, 'You went for platinum blonde', because that's the wig he was wearing.

"And then after the show he usually stops by our table and chats a little bit, but this time he came by, collected his forty bucks, and he was out of there. So I don't know if that was a message, or a reaction to that Dave completed the kiss? Or if it was just because he was quite high?"

"I think he was out of it," April continued. "He was slurring his words a little bit, and wrote on one of his social media pages that, before the show, he had taken a bit too much edibles.

"Anyway, Dave couldn't sleep. We're in different rooms right now because I'm sleeping on the floor with the dog, and Dave comes in, and it's really early morning, so I said, 'What's going on?' And he said, 'I just can't sleep.' And I told him, 'It's the kiss, right?' And he goes, 'Yes, it's the kiss.'"

"So what about the kiss?" Carl asked.

I said it was unexpected and felt as though it would be seared in my memory forever – Parted purple lips the only thing I could see, and then the questions of what it meant after?

"It means you enjoyed a kiss," Carl asserted...

CHAPTER SEVENTY-NINE

"You have been seduced."

April and I sat talking over lunch.

"I am not immune to his charms," she continued, "but I haven't been taken in emotionally. He either does not have a romantic partner, or is not that active sexually, or he's very private about it, because he talks about a whole lot of other stuff, but he doesn't ever really mention that."

This surprised me, being I imagined him a good lover.

"Because of the kiss?" she asked.

Yes. Where he'd intentionally made his lips soft, it led me to feel he'd be gentle.

I shook my head. Never in my fifty-five years had I entertained such thoughts.

"I was wondering," April said. "When you kissed him, did you have an erection?"

No, for me it's not about sex or eroticism or excitement. It's about tenderness. It's about affection.

"Did you feel chemistry, though, when you kissed him?"

No, I don't know what he feels.

She commented about my seeming ready acceptance of Mercury's smoking and cannabis use.

"If I did that, you'd be like, 'I'm divorcing you'," she said. "But when Mercury does it, you say, 'It's funny.'"

She was alluding to a video Mercury posted in which he took a hit of marijuana, then made his image go sideways.

"Like he can do no wrong," she contended. "Except for rejecting you…"

CHAPTER EIGHTY

Considering the night's events, it struck me that I could have given Mercury my cheek (as he'd done to me) and in advancing as I had, I'd been the instigator.

"I don't think you were the 'instigator'," April responded. "I think you were the 'completer'."

I nodded, appreciating the break.

"Do you think he kept his eyes open?" she asked.

I didn't know. From the moment he moved towards me, all I could see were his lips.

"Big, gigantic, blue lips coming towards you," she accented. "Have you ever kissed blue lips before?"

No. Hence, it was a first in more ways than one.

"How long was it?"

I crossed the table at the restaurant where we'd been sitting and demonstrated.

"OK, if he didn't want it, he would have moved."

The way he walked by me at the end of the show, I'd say he didn't care.

"The way I read it, it was a signal. A woman would do that... A woman with someone who maybe she just wants to be friends with, but they've crossed a little line, so that she's giving you a message: 'I like you, but it felt a little weird, so I'm going to chill out a little bit, so that maybe you'll chill down, and we can both take a deep breath.' Give you a little bit of a cold shoulder, so that you get the hint, and you'll stay friends. I read it like, 'We went a little bit further than I intended, and I need to re-establish a boundary.' That's what a woman would do. Like, 'I like you, but I'm not ready for that right now.'..."

CHAPTER EIGHTY-ONE

Reclining in the cushioned chair I reflected on how I'd unmasked myself in public.

"In front of Julie and Jeb," April inserted. "Did Jeb catch that?... That you went for it?"

I couldn't imagine he hadn't.

"How much did you move?"

I demonstrated.

"And it was that soft?... Do it again."

I complied. She laughed.

"Can you do it again?" she asked, sweetly.

Reminding her we were in a public place, I returned to my side of the table.

"How did he take the money at the end of the night?" she asked.

I held it out, and he took it and kept walking.

"How does he take money from you during the show?"

He usually holds my hand before he removes the bills.

Nodding, April took a dollar from her purse.

"Show me how he does it," she said.

I demonstrated.

"So he massages your hand each time?"

Yes.

She gave me the dollar.

"This is how he takes it from me," she said.

She pulled the dollar from my hand with no contact...

CHAPTER EIGHTY-TWO

I confided that I hadn't gone to Badlands last night because I was afraid more might come of it.

"What do you mean?" April asked. "That he might come after you?"

I sighed. Put that way, my reservations sounded like the very height of vanity.

But, yes, I was afraid.

"I think Mercury is a flirt," she commented, "so that you can send him code words, like a pre-prepared joke that would call it out."

I didn't want to joke. And I didn't want to hold back. I just didn't know what I wanted.

She nodded.

"So this chain smoker. Heavy pot smoker. Probably gets up at one in the afternoon and goes to sleep at three in the morning. You'd have to change so much of your life – what you're about – to be with him."

It didn't make sense. I wasn't homosexual. I wasn't even bi.

"But this is what I've been trying to say – Trying to convince you... To keep it light. And fun. And flirty."

Yes, but the problem is, I'm in love.

She laughed.

"Lord!" she blurted. *"Born to be Wild* – 'You can go so high' – What's the next part?"

'I never want to die.'

I'd been denying it. She, on the other hand, always knew.

"I know puppy love when I see it," she responded. "You just look at him, and you have this puppy love face."

"The problem with puppy love," she added, "is it can be very painful."

She covered her lips.

"Sorry I laughed before," she said. "I couldn't help it."

How could it not be funny? A straight man in love with a drag queen.

"A gay guy," she added. "You don't even know his legal name. Is it fun?"

Loads, especially when he walks on by, I said with sweeping hand motion.

"Ohhh, that's not funny!" she cried, full of warmth and caring. "Here!" She crossed the table and held me. "Puppy love pains…"

CHAPTER EIGHTY-THREE

After next week's show April said she had an idea and asked me to request Katy Perry's *I Kissed a Girl* for karaoke.

"But in this version," she asserted with mischievous smile, "replace the word 'girl' with 'queen', 'cherry chapstick' with 'lime lipstick', and 'boyfriend' with 'wife'."

As I stood onstage about to start, April pulled Mercury aside and asked him to watch.

I kissed a queen and I liked it.
The taste of her lime lipstick.
I kissed a queen just to try it.
I hope my wife don't mind it.

As I sang, Mercury removed his winter cap, applied a blond wig and lip-synced along.

It felt so wrong.
It felt so right.
Don't mean I'm in love tonight.
I kissed a queen and I liked it.
I liked it...

Arriving at the song's end Mercury pulled off the wig and lifted both arms and cheered...

"When you were singing that part, 'I hope my wife don't mind it'," April confided later, "he turned to me and said, 'Do you mind?'

"I was filming at the time, going back-and-forth between you two, and too star-struck to say anything.

"Now, I think I would have stroked his hand like he does to you, and said, 'Sweetie, I don't mind. I think it's hot.'..."

CHAPTER EIGHTY-FOUR

April and I returned to The Depot for the another installment of *RuPaul's Drag Race* and watch-party. But unlike other times, we were treated to a free pass to the front – like the Red Sea were parting before us.

"I think people are used to seeing us," April said, "and treating us with more respect..."

In this week's program the drag queen contestants were tasked with putting together a dance number. In the process one of the drag queens was criticized for being less than eager to hit the floor during dance practice, and later explained it was because she had a rare connective tissue disorder that left her with a predisposition for joint dislocation.

"I don't know about you guys," Mercury called out during the commercial break, "but it feels like this season is more and more like fucking *Grey's Anatomy.*"

April turned.

"I didn't like that," she said. "That drag queen wasn't making excuses – She was simply saying why she couldn't do that."

I agreed, though it didn't dim my appreciation for Mercury at all. Indeed, his example was pushing me to improve: Over the past weeks that April had been taking photographs of me in drag, I'd been scrutinizing my posture, working out the kinks in my neck and shoulders and standing taller and straighter than I ever had.

But chasing after Mercury was like trying to keep up with a moving target, as every week his physique was changing, becoming more sculpted (or, as he would say, 'ripped'), like an chiseled rendering of Adonis.

"Mercury is really good about having a straight vertebrae and squared shoulders," April responded. "I think from there everything flows, like stability and ability to do the amazing things he does."

"But you're the one with the body of a Greek youth," she asserted. "You have well-defined muscles. You're lean. That's what they looked like in the drawings of them on the walls and ceramic jars."

Mercury has lean, well-defined muscles, I countered. It's just that he so much taller than I am.

"But your shoulders are wider than his!" she insisted. "His shoulders are narrow. His bones are narrow. It's like he's Gumby and somebody stretched him. SHHHKKK!"

"And you have an extra gene," she added, "that makes certain parts of you wide. And he doesn't have that. It's almost like you had a giant for an ancestor somewhere in your line, and what you got from that was your feet, hands and penis."

Indeed, April did seem ever more pleased with my physique of late: Earlier in the week she'd brought home a 'pencil dress' and liked the way it fit me.

"There are very few people – women included – who can rock a pencil dress!" she declared. "You have to have a perfect body to rock this dress. It's a testament to all of the hard work and physical conditioning you've put in to take care of your body…"

At the conclusion of the *RuPaul* episode, the crowd pressed in to watch Mercury and Aurora take turns dancing. Those in attendance consisted of mostly young men who stood a full head taller than me, so that it seemed unlikely I was going to see anything. But April took my hand and slid us into the front.

Aurora was first this time. Her slender, angular frame was capable of movement so fast as to somehow defy visual perception. Liquid and fluid and radiant, watching her was like looking upon fire. Throughout life I prided myself on being able to get in touch with my feminine side when dancing; but compared to her, I hadn't even touched the surface.

Just then, Aurora turned and was heading right towards me. She was no doubt looking to head into the crowd to collect tips from the outstretched hands of those behind me. But the speed of her approach left me frozen (like the proverbial 'deer in the headlights'), awaiting impact.

But no collision happened; Aurora just pivoted and delicately passed me, so that I only experienced the slightest of touch upon my shoulder.

Once again, there was nothing to fear, and watching her make her way into the crowd, I considered the difference between she and I. In most ways I was a pretty conventional guy. I'd lived in a small town in Tennessee for years with Kate and the kids, and got along just fine. I probably still could, and no one was going to give me a hard time about who I was. Whereas I didn't think that would be the case for Aurora....

Mercury was next. During his number he too left the dance circle, as he sure-footedly climbed atop a barstool and crossed onto the bar. But when he performed a seated spin on the counter, he wound up in puddle of spilled beer that seeped through his clothing. Looking back at the wet spot on his garment, he seemed at a loss for what to do. Urging him on, April broke with tradition (i.e., her pattern of foregoing tipping) and held out several dollar bills. Taking them from her, Mercury invited April to dance.

"That was quite sweet of him," April commented. "Maybe it's because he feels guilty."

In my dreams, I responded, skeptically...

But wilder dreams were yet to come.

As usual, rather than just pull the bills from my outstretched hand, Mercury held my fingers for a while, caressing them.

And then it happened: During the night I considered how I'd enjoyed his touch and for the first time experienced arousal...

CHAPTER EIGHTY-FIVE

"What makes Mercury different from your other guy friends?" April asked.

Mercury didn't put his arms around me and pull me into a bear hug like the way, say, Dino does, I responded (Though, truth-be-told, Dino hadn't done that since the night at the Capitol Garage); instead, it's this light touch.

"But why can't a guy be sweet like that?" she asked. "Is it not something that a guy's supposed to be?"

Yes, but there's this duality about him: On the one hand, he has this intense male strength; on the other, a femininity that reaches me to the core.

"He's two-spirited!" she declared, emphatically. "That's why I think it's wrong to refer to him as 'him' all the time. I know he's capable of being tough – the way he was when he got that homeless man out of the restaurant – but, really, I think he is he/she, in that he is both a he and a she…"

CHAPTER EIGHTY-SIX

"One of the things that is bothering me," April told Carl, "is Dave refuses to call Mercury, 'Her.' He always talks about Mercury as a 'He.' And that bothers me. That he has feelings for her, but doesn't refer to her as a 'her'."

"There are so many variants on this," Carl responded. "I know several people who are transitioning, and some of them – essentially the males transitioning to females – they really want to be called 'She'. But they're transitioning. They don't have that guise. And I don't see Mercury as transsexual. Or transgender. Or Trans anything. Really, I see Mercury as throwing things out as Mercury. And I don't know if that's as a 'he' or a 'she' or the more and more common usage of 'they'."

"Yeah, but it actually got me mad," April admitted. "It makes me mad for Mercury. Because I think Dave should be respecting Mercury as a character. And I know that when you talk to the staff members at The Capitol Garage about Mercury, they always refer to Mercury as female. They always say, 'Oh, she's not here', or, 'She will be performing.' I think they know him also as a male, but I know when they're referring to Mercury, they refer to her as a female."

"You are bringing up something really interesting," Carl responded. "Because Mercury as 'Mercury' – as the performer 'Mercury' – you're saying she should be identified as 'she'. It's only when Mercury is out of costume that he should be referred to as 'he'."

"The question is," April asserted. "Within his community, the fact that his super fan sees him as male, instead of as a female, would that be considered a failing on his part? As a female impersonator? That would be my question – Would that be one of the things he gets judged on? Or are they just open, and everybody can do what they have to do, and express whatever they want? That's where I'm coming from – Is it being disrespectful?'"

"And I imagine that Mercury would say, 'How do you perceive me? – That's what this should be about,'" Carl countered.

Still, April wasn't satisfied.

"I know Dave feels very strongly about calling him a 'he'," she said, "because for Dave he's a 'he'."

But this wasn't entirely true: The more I interacted with Mercury, the more he became a 'she' to me. The other night Mercury approached me from behind and greeted me by clasping his hands on my shoulders; and it was that light touch, and liked it and eased into it, signaling to me that I was coming to accept, respect, appreciate and even desire this person as a feminine being.

"The thing that grabbed me from the start," I said, "was this powerful male danseur. That's the Mercury I saw the first time. But with time I have been bringing his feminine qualities in, so that – at the very least – I do see him as 'two-spirited', and am quite losing myself in the whole he/she nature of things."

"Of course you are," Carl responded, understandingly. "Because if Mercury was a 'she', there would be no issue. Then, you would just be attracted to a woman. But Mercury being a 'he' is what puts all the tension in it…"

CHAPTER EIGHTY-SEVEN

"I don't know," my friend Ben responded to the question of my feelings for Mercury and what that might mean to my marriage. "I've been monogamous with Michele since we've been together, and I could never share that with anyone else – Simply because of the depth of it. But that's me. I don't know your and April's relationship. That's between the two of you. You may both be wanderers?... You may both like to wander?

"Honestly, it sounds like something in your spirit has been stirred. That's the spirit. The spirit is connected with everybody around you and everything. And it might be more, but it doesn't have to."

"Maybe the lesson is," he concluded, "that you have to let your spirit out..."

CHAPTER EIGHTY-EIGHT

April overheard me telling Ben about her comments regarding Mercury's smoking and wanted to clarify.

"It wasn't anything against Mercury," she began. "I was just reacting to the fact that you told me the night before I got married to you – or, I don't know, maybe sometime before – that if I ever started smoking that was grounds for divorce. But here you are interested in a person who is an unabashed smoker. That was basically what the comment was about. That was me saying, 'You're really changing yourself for him – or her.'

"Because you were obviously attracted to me, too. You wouldn't have married me if there wasn't something pulling you towards me. But here you are following a smoker like the Pied Piper. You are willing to throw out your deeply held convictions – just burn them up – because you are so attracted to him. That's how strong the attraction is. And that's what I meant when I said you're changing who you are. You're changing your lifestyle. You're changing all these things about you in the hope of being with him. You're saying, 'To be with him is more important than any of these other things.'"

Yes, it would seem I've changed.

"What?!" she responded, touched and smiling. "If I were to start smoking now, you wouldn't divorce me?!"

She laughed, and I edged closer.

When we got back together, I said, I'd just left a difficult relationship – a person I'd loved and lied to me. And if there was something I wanted after that, it was someone I could trust. That's why I reached out to you. You were the only person I could imagine fully trusting.

"What was it about me that made you think I was trustworthy?"

164

In the short time we'd known each other all those years ago, I got the feeling that I knew her heart. I believed in her honesty, and thought that she liked me.

She nodded.

"You know, not long after my grandfather died, I asked my grandmother, 'Would you consider dating again?' And she looked at me and she said something to the effect of, 'Generally, when people date at my age, mostly it's people that they knew previously when they were younger. But everyone that I knew previously when I was younger is dead.' So, she basically said, 'I might be interested in dating some of my old friends, but I'm not interested in somebody completely new.'"

Yes, that's where I was back then. But it seems I'm in a different place now, whether because I've recovered, or become more mature, or...

"Or simply forgotten," she inserted.

Any of those things, I conceded.

The other night a drag queen performed a number that included the line, "You always like to play – But you never want to lose." That was me, I said. I had played and lost – and then withdrew. But I'm not avoiding now. Not anything or anyone. I'm ready to engage.

"Do you think that that woman coming on to you was like a little turning point or something?" April asked.

Yes, the fact that I could stand my ground and this woman still engage me (even when she wasn't getting what she wanted) and let her guard down and laugh so comfortably in response to that last thing I said – Yes, I enjoyed that – Like being friendly was fun...

"From the get go," I admitted, "me looking for you was conditional. I was looking for someone I could trust. As opposed to Mercury – who I wasn't looking for – who came from out of the blue. Where it just happened – and for whatever reason (whether because of his dancing, or his warmth, and the effect it had on me, and the endorphins in my brain) there's been something unconditional to it – such that all manner of pretense and precondition has gone away."

"But is that healthy?" she asked.

I shrugged.

It just is, I responded.

"Because if he says, yes, and now you're in a relationship with him, will you still be able to tolerate smoke in the house?" she queried.

I shook my head.

All I know of him is as a performer, I said. I don't know the real person. And it might be that the only way I'd want him is in the makeup and outfits and wigs. What kind of relationship would that be? If you asked me, it sounds awful.

"So it's not so un-con-di-tion-al," she teased. "And he knows it."

Whether he knows it or not, I think I can do best by him by supporting what he does.

"I know I love him as an artist," I said. "I think that's where it's healthiest…"

CHAPTER EIGHTY-NINE

A red and bumpy rash across my forehead (No doubt an allergic reaction to the wigs) seemed to signal the end of my drag fun. Between that and my intolerance to hair dyes, it just felt like the universe was insistent I be as I am.

So, on Saturday, I arrived at the Capitol Garage, wigless.

Mercury, meanwhile, was outfitted all in blue (from wig to lipstick to backless dress), delighting the crowd with his electric dancing. Even April was uncharacteristically inspired to hold out a few dollar bills to him – And taking them from her, April turned to me, delightedly laughing.

"He massaged *my hand* this time!" she exclaimed.

Most notable about the evening, however, was Mercury's interactions with children. Removing his wig after a particularly strenuous dance number, Mercury casually plopped it on the head of a child.

"Hold this," he said. "I'm getting too hot."

The little boy, laughing, turned to his parents – the light sparkling from the wig that now hung from his head.

My mind flashed to that day at LAX with my grandparents, and the thought that (had he been there) Mercury would have surely won over my disparaging mother...

Lucy Ludicrus was the other drag queen performing, and, as usual, she put a temporary halt to the dancing – this time to query the audience as to their sexual orientation?

"How many are straight?!" Ludicrus called out.

When I didn't self-identify, April looked at me.

"Why didn't you respond?" she asked.

I said that given the happenings of the past weeks and months, I'd rather come to question.

"How many out there are bi?!" Ludicrus continued.

"Are you bi?" April asked.

I shook my head.

I don't think so, I responded. I'd say I'm more a 'Mercuro-sexual.'

"That's 'pansexual' I believe," she asserted. "That's when you're attracted to the person. So you say, 'I don't care about the gender, I just care about the person.'"

I nodded.

Sounds right, I said.

"But that's not entirely right, because you do care about the gender," she commented, "and the fact that he is a male is taking you on a loop."

"Oh, you guys who are bi just want everyone!" Ludicrus called out, feigning exasperation.

"What would you prefer?" April asked. "To be pansexual over bisexual?"

Yes, because I had no interest in guys outside of Mercury.

"How about Ben?"

Ben is my friend. I don't want to have sex with him. For that matter, I don't want to have sex with any of my male friends, or any men in general.

"But the really big question I want to know," Mercury interrupted, "is how many here are under ten?!"

Shouts came from all sides of the Capitol Garage, and Mercury and Ludicrus spontaneously broke into song, singing the *Baby Shark* song as they pranced between tables, the children delighting in their hand gestures, and everyone in the establishment joining in...

At the end of the show, as Mercury took selfies with adoring fans of all ages, April asked if I'd given up on Mercury and would look for someone else?

No, I said. Mercury was truly one in a billion; he'd be the one man on the planet I'd ever experience such feelings, and who in the process taught me something about the power of love – That love makes all things possible.

"How do you know that?" she asked. "Now that you found such feelings, you might find someone else you like?"

Sure, I responded. Anything's possible...

Requesting Chicago's *Beginnings* for karaoke, I sang of the charge of love.

When I'm with you-ou-ou,
It doesn't matter where we are.

Mercury came walking towards the stage as I sang. A father holding his toddler son was standing nearby, and Mercury interacted sweetly with the child, making faces and speaking in a high-pitched voice, as the child squealed in delight.

Kids should see this type of thing, I thought. They should be open to other ways of living. Of loving. So to learn tolerance from an early age. To understand that we're all people, in spite of any difference in sexual orientation or anything else. That more than the color of one's skin or their sexual orientation is the love that person puts out in the world...

As I finished the song, Mercury stood alongside April, applauding.

"Maybe one day I'll be your backup singer?" he joked, hugging me.

Handing him our usual contribution, I told him it was we who wanted to back him up.

He shrugged.

"Well, I try," he said, humbly.

You succeed! I responded, emphatically...

After Mercury went back to his dressing room, it struck April that she wanted to catch him before we left and stood by his door. When he reappeared (now out of costume), she approached him...

"I told him, 'Thank you'," she related. "That we both have been on this journey of exploration and discovery, and I've been experimenting with makeup, and Dave's been experimenting with clothes.

"I said I'd be away for a while. That the dog was having surgery, and I was going to be staying home on Saturday nights, instead of coming. But that you'd be coming. So he said, 'Well, he could take lots of videos for you.'

"I just didn't want him to have a feeling like I didn't want to be here anymore. I was kind of saying goodbye to people. I also told the DJ, and he said he would make sure you had fun."

"So, I gave him forewarning that the cat's going to be away," she said with impish grin. "We'll see if he doesn't act a little bit more risqué when you're there by yourself.

"You got to tell me everything. Because I'm going to want to know. It would be so hot if you guys… Oh my God. I hope it doesn't bother you that I find it hot."

No, I was just happy to be with someone willing to go down an unexpected road with me.

Mercury passed as he made his way out.

"Good luck," he told April.

Then, he stopped alongside me.

"I love you, I love you," he said, indicating his cheek...

"Did you hear that?!" April asked, excited. "He said, 'I love you!'"

Yes, I heard.

That's what he does. He gives love.

And that's why I support him.

And love him, too…

David Fischer MD PhD is a
Professor of Medicine who cares for the
homeless, leads efforts to combat the opioid crisis and
advances integrative therapies for the treatment of pain.

Mercury Rising was voted
Best Drag Queen in Sacramento.

He still performs at the Capitol Garage.

www.ingramcontent.com/pod-product-compliance
Lightning Source LLC
Chambersburg PA
CBHW032111280326
41933CB00009B/788